# MILLER'S

# silver &
# sheffield
# plate marks

including a guide to
makers and styles

## Miller's Silver & Sheffield Plate Marks

### John Bly

First published in Great Britain in 1993 by
Miller's, a division of Mitchell Beazley, both
imprints of Octopus Publishing Group Ltd,
2–4 Heron Quays, London E14 4JP
Miller's is a registered trademark of
Octopus Publishing Group Ltd,
an Hachette Livre UK company.

A CIP catalogue record for this book is available
from the British Library.

ISBN  9781 84533 348 5

Set in ITC Galliard & News Gothic
Colour origination in China by Sang Choy
Printed and bound in China by Toppan

**Managing Editor** Valerie Lewis
**Project Editor** MiniMel Smith
**Copy Editor** Jo Thom
**Designers** Mark Winwood, Angel Design & Print
**Editorial Assistants** Caroline Bugeja,
    Ethne Tragett, Alexandra Lewis-Wortley
**Marks Artwork** Ian Lamont
**Indexer** Hilary Bird
**Production** Peter Hunt
**Photography** Robin Saker, Paul Harding

# MILLER'S

# silver & sheffield plate marks

## including a guide to makers and styles

John Bly

# Contents

# FOREWORD

JOHN BLY

Antique silver is tangible history. It is a tactile art form, and there is no better way of learning than by touch; hence the most important part of the education of the collector is the handling of as much silver as possible.

Feel how the silversmith has beaten life into his element. Feel the edges, the surface, the top and beneath. Before established collectors raise their hands in horror, I should add that, if the silver is valuable or rare, cotton gloves should be worn. Look obliquely against the light and see the myriad of tiny scratches that produce an unfakeable patina or 'skin', which has resulted from years of gentle use and care. Put yourself in the place of the silversmith and imagine how he fashioned the piece. If you are lucky enough to have inherited some silver, get to know it well; otherwise look in salerooms or antiques shops.

When you have decided where your interest lies, then venture forth and buy – modestly at first. There are bound to be fakes and alterations in any field today, but the silver collector has the hallmarking system as a guard, and auctioneers, art dealers and other collectors are all surprisingly keen to advise and impart knowledge, not only to make a sale, but to encourage another member to the circle of silver devotees.

Although silver was first marked in 1300, the vast majority of marked wares seen on the market today date from the turn of the 17th century. Hence, the majority of marks listed in this book span from this date up to c1939, thus covering the most important collecting period for silver. Some marks may stop earlier if an office closed down before 1939 and, in the case of major towns, later marks have sometimes been included.

*Miller's Silver and Sheffield Plate Marks* has proved to be a popular guide for the novice collector and a useful source of reference for those already experienced in the field.

# INTRODUCTION

For the purposes of this book, the term 'silver' refers to items made from silver metal which, from medieval times, provided the coin of the realm of England, and the raw material for objects both decorative and domestic.

In its pure form, silver is too soft for normal use and it must be mixed (alloyed) with a hardening agent (alloy), predominately copper. Once alloyed, the metal is beaten out with a hammer, a hardening process called annealing. The silversmith must take care not to hit the same spot twice until the piece has been heated to realign the structure of the atoms, which are then restored to a state to withstand more beating. In this way, as a potter raises his pot and a cook his pastry, a silversmith raises his ware.

From the earliest times, objects made from silver were produced on a large scale and, as there was no standard of silver content, the description 'silver' could be misleading. Early silverwares were often referred to as 'wrought plate' (plate used here in the sense simply of 'wares') and consisted of silver alloyed with copper. Copper was an ideal hardening agent because it did not affect the colour of the silver. It was, however, impossible to assess the purity or percentage alloy of silver with the naked eye, and the unscrupulous silversmith could add excess copper without fear of detection.

## THE SILVER STANDARD

In times of affluence a hoard of coinage could be transformed into decorative or useful silver wares, whilst in hard times such silver wares could be melted down to produce currency. It was only when goods were melted down that the dishonesty of unscrupulous silversmiths became apparent.

A system of testing was required whereby adulterated silver could be identified without melting down the objects made from it. The 'touch' process then in use for testing gold, involved the scraping of the metal on a touchstone; the streaks left behind were compared to the streaks left by a piece of true gold. However, this system was insufficient for testing silver as even adulterated metal was the same colour throughout. A more accurate test was required.

A process was therefore developed that involved the weighing and heating of a scraping (slither or scroll) of silver in a cup of bone ash. Any copper component was absorbed into the bone ash, leaving a nugget of pure silver which was also weighed; the difference between the two weights gave a percentage adulteration. In 1300 a mark was introduced, to be applied to silverwares tested for quality (assayed). Only silver containing at least 925 parts of silver per thousand (92.5%) to 75 parts of copper (7.5%)

could be termed 'sterling' and receive an official stamp, or mark, as guarantee. Marking also made it easier for customs officials to prevent the export of silver from England. The stamp, known as the 'King's mark', represented a lion's head. This motif was called a 'leopart' in the heraldic French then in usage with the educated classes, and has become the leopard's head of today. Fable has it that the

Leopard's head

standard was introduced at the command of King John by a group of German silversmiths. The Germans were historically one of the Continental races referred to by the British as Easterlings, and the standard became known as the 'easterling standard', which was

corrupted to esterling and, supposedly, to sterling. On 30 March 1327, a charter was introduced by Edward III, giving royal acknowledgment to the Worshipful Company of Goldsmiths, and bestowing the right to conduct and enforce the assay laws. As assaying was to be carried out at Goldsmiths' Hall, the headquarters of the guild, the mark of guarantee was referred to as a 'hallmark'. The crown on the leopard's head was removed in 1821/22.

Until 1378, assay was carried out only at Goldsmiths' Hall in London and all silver had to be taken there for testing to gain the king's mark. The person was elected on an annual basis to supervise the assay and he was called the master of touch, assay master, or touch warden.

Silversmiths were often reluctant to bring their wares over long distances to London for assay. Transport in the 14th century was slow, uncomfortable and fraught with danger. Many silversmiths preferred to ignore the law and to sell their wares unmarked rather than embark on such a journey. Also, it is probable that a dishonest minority in the provinces continued to produce and sell substandard wares. This dissension threatened to undermine the guarantee of the Goldsmiths' Company; hence, in 1363, the powers of touch were granted to mayors of all cities and boroughs, whereby a representative was elected to carry out the functions of the London office in situ.

Prior to c1350 few, if any, makers had marked their wares with an identifying device and a means was required by which an individual maker could be traced, should his wares prove substandard at assay. Thus, also in 1363, the maker's mark was legislated. As literacy was still the province of the church and the educated few, initials could not be read by the majority of the population, so simple pictorial representations were used. These were usually based on a relevant symbol, perhaps a pun on the silversmith's name or a motif taken from his shop sign.

**THE SILVER STANDARD**

1721  1741  1781  1801

After the introduction, in 1363, of powers of touch to the mayors of all cities and boroughs, it became necessary to introduce a system to make the master of touch personally responsible for maintaining the silver standard. The master was re-elected annually, so from 1478 in London, silver was marked with a different letter of the alphabet each year. When the alphabet was exhausted, either the style of the letter or the form of the shield background was altered and the alphabetical cycle began again. Other town and city assay offices subsequently followed suit and introduced similar date letter marks.

By the beginning of the 16th century, although the standard of wrought plate was well-established, the nation's coinage (supposedly of sterling silver) had become debased. The Goldsmiths' Company decided to establish their own guarantee of quality and in 1544 the lion passant mark was introduced, showing a lion seen full-figure in

Lion passant    York    Exeter    Edinburgh

profile, looking over its shoulder and waving. This fast replaced the leopard's head as the sterling mark. The leopard's head became increasingly recognized as the London mark when other cities adopted their own assay marks. In York, a mark was adopted in 1560, described at the time as 'the pounce of this citie, called the halfe leopard head and halfe flowre-de-luyce' (half leopard, half fleur-de-lys). Other cities to adopt marks at an early stage were Exeter (their cross with a crown was first used in 1575) and Edinburgh (a castle, first used in 1556). However, as the Goldsmiths' guarantee of quality, the lion passant was used by several provincial assay offices, including York, Newcastle, Chester, Exeter and Bristol, in conjunction with their own town mark.

## MILLING AND THE BRITANNIA SILVER STANDARD

Until the reign of Charles II, the silver coin of the realm was hand-made and stamped. However, by the time of the Restoration the practice of 'clipping' was rife. Clipping involved paring a minute piece of silver from the edge of coins until a sizeable hoard of silver was amassed, which could be forged into home-made coinage, or (since this offence was punishable by death) the stolen silver clippings were sometimes sold to a silversmith. To prevent clipping, the government had, by 1697, issued coinage with a milled edge and withdrawn the old clipped coins from circulation. In order to render silver clippings useless to a silversmith, the silver standard was raised from 925 parts per thousand (92.5%) to a purer 958.4 (95.84%), the

Lion's Head

Britannia

highest possible silver content before the metal became unworkably soft. This new standard was denoted by two new marks, which replaced the leopard's head and lion passant; these were the lion's head erased (in heraldic terms meaning 'torn from the shoulders'), still in profile, and the figure of Britannia. The new standard was therefore called the Britannia silver standard.

The increased purity of silver meant that the metal was softer and as a result different shapes began to appear (see Silver Styles, pp89–91). The new metal could no longer support the thinly-gauged, embossed and repoussé decorations popular during the Restoration, and these were replaced by more heavily-gauged forms. Items were more often cast and chased as well as engraved, and raised wares were of simple shape; thus domestic silver tended to be either extremely plain or highly decorated.

This new style of silver manufacture was already popular in France, where Huguenot silversmiths were used to working with higher quality silver. Following the Revocation of the Edict of Nantes in 1685, hoards of French protestants fled religious persecution in France and large numbers of Huguenot craftsmen settled in Great Britain, where they practised their craft and spread their skills amongst the British.

The Britannia standard remained legal and obligatory until June 1720, when the sterling standard was reinstated by popular demand and the old sterling marks were once more used. The Britannia standard had proved comparatively expensive for both maker and buyer and had bankrupted many smaller silversmiths now consigned to the oblivion of undocumented history. Nevertheless it remained, and remains today, a legal option, although it is

Amyé Videau

Paul Storr c1792–1834

not in common use. By the middle of the 17th century, the continued development of trade, commerce and a middle class led to vast growth in learning, and literacy was no longer the preserve of a few. From 1720 the maker's mark incorporated letters rather than a symbol. To begin with the first two letters of the maker's surname were used, but after a few years their initials were adopted.

By 1720, a hallmarking system was in operation that offered a reliable guarantee to the buying public. An indication of its effectiveness is that, today, we can tell who made a piece, what it is made of, where it was assayed and by whom, and the year of assay. It was, and still is, the most comprehensive recognition system in the world. Although the basic system has remained unchanged for over 270 years, other marks have come and gone. On 1 December 1784, a tax was imposed on silver, which at one time was recorded as reaching the punitive rate of 6d an ounce. The tax was collected by the Commissioners of

| George III<br>1784–85 | George III<br>1785–1820 | Victoria<br>1837–90 |

Stamps, the forerunners of today's Inland Revenue. Intended as a temporary duty, it was to last for 106 years, finally being abolished in 1890. To signify payment of this tax, a mark was introduced showing the sovereign's head in profile. For the first year this mark was intaglio (indented) in complete reverse of all other marks, which were struck in cameo. From 1 January 1785, it too changed to become a cameo mark. As the assay master's mark changed in May each year, those pieces stamped in the first half of 1785 can be traced to that six-month period exactly, an unusual level of precision. Such pieces are popular with certain collectors, although this mark does not in itself add much to the value of a piece of silver.

From 1784 until 1890, five marks appeared on English silver (sterling, town, date, maker, sovereign's head). From 1891 until today only four marks are used on most English silver of the sterling or Britannia standard (sterling, town, date, maker). There are three exceptions: the Jubilee mark used on pieces assayed in 1934–35 in honour of the Silver

| Jubilee<br>1934–35 | Coronation<br>1952–53 | Silver Jubilee<br>1977 |

Jubilee of King George V and Queen Mary; the Coronation mark, used on pieces assayed in 1953, the year of Queen Elizabeth II's coronation; and the Silver Jubilee mark, an optional mark appearing on some items of over 15 grams in weight produced in 1977, the year of the Silver Jubilee of Queen Elizabeth II's accession.

## CONVENTION MARKS

From 1 June 1976, some special marks used at certain assay offices in the United Kingdom, Austria, Denmark, Finland, Ireland, Norway, Portugal, Sweden and Switzerland became legally acceptable under an international convention. These include a fineness mark (Arabic numerals showing the standard in parts per

Common
control
mark

thousand), a sponsor's mark, a common control mark and an assay office mark. Marks for the common European silver standard of 800 and 830 parts per thousand are also included, but these are not approved legal standards for articles sold in Britain.

## THE HALLMARKING ACT OF 1973

The Hallmarking Act of 1973 rationalized many of the anomalies that existed in hallmarking law, although the silver standards remain unchanged. Each piece of silver must now be stamped with a sponsor's mark (this has largely replaced the maker's mark and shows the person responsible for manufacturing the piece), a standard mark, an assay office mark and a date letter. The standard marks are now identical at all four assay offices, except in the case of sterling silver, where the Edinburgh assay office uses a lion rampant in place of the lion passant used by the English offices.

## SCOTTISH AND IRISH SILVER

To a large extent, Scottish and Irish silver share a history, in that both have their very early roots in the ecclesiastical silver of the Celtic church.

However, by the 12th century the Norman influence had pervaded Scotland and the prevailing taste was for artefacts in the Romanesque style. In 1457, James II of Scotland set a standard for silver of no less than eleven parts out of twelve (the equivalent of 916 parts per thousand). He also legislated a maker's mark and the mark of the dene or deacon, the chief office bearer of his craft in a town and the equivalent to the English assay master. Being an active gold or silversmith, the deacon's personal mark would be used for the duration of his tenure of office; hence a piece of this date could appear to bear two makers' marks. By 1483, a guild system had been established, with Scottish gold and silversmiths in company with other hammermen (craftsmen whose work entailed the use of a hammer) as there were not enough silversmiths to form their own substantial company. Also by 1483, the town mark was in use.

Scotland's turbulent relationship with England meant that the country's gold and, to a lesser extent, its silver, was often plundered or confiscated and not many early wares survive. It is also likely that a substantial amount was destroyed during the Reformation, and the Catholic Mary Queen of Scots melted down the rest in 1567, as a result of her strife with John Knox, her Presbyterian adversary.

Edinburgh
from 1485

In 1617, the Scottish Parliament decreed that all parishes should be equipped with the basic utensils necessary for a communion service; this date marks the beginning of comprehensive documentation of silverwares in Scotland.

However, Scottish secular plate is exceptionally rare until the second half of the 17th century. In 1681, a cycle of date letters was introduced that remains in use today, and in the same year the deacon's mark was replaced by the assay master's mark.

Following the Act of Union with Scotland of 1603, the re-introduction of sterling silver into England in 1720 meant that Scottish silversmiths had also to raise their silver

1759–1975  from 1975
Edinburgh

standard, but this made no difference to their marking system. In 1759, the thistle mark replaced the assay master's mark, which was in turn replaced by the lion rampant in 1975. Otherwise, from the second half of the 18th century, the duty marks and optional marks used in Scotland follow those used in England.

Dublin  Hibernia

In Ireland, from 1637, silver was marked with an assay mark depicting a crowned harp. This stamp was also used as a Dublin town mark 1637–1807. After 1807 a stamp showing the seated figure of Hibernia was used as Dublin's town mark.

## UNMARKED WARES

Over the centuries, a number of parliamentary acts in Great Britain have made it illegal to sell unmarked wares as silver, gold or platinum. However, there is in existence a substantial number of wares made before 1900 that are incompletely marked or not marked at all. There are several possible reasons for this. The piece may be part of a larger set produced strictly to commission and marked only on one piece. Alternatively, it could be part of a multi-piece item; for example, a candleholder that would originally have been attached to an inkwell. Or it could simply be too small to mark. Until 1973, it was considered that any unmarked piece offered for sale should be assayed and marked. As a result some unmarked, genuine pieces were sent to assay and given modern marks which effectively destroyed any aspect of their historical importance. However, modern science has perfected the spectrographic test, whereby the precise age of a piece can be ascertained, and the assay law has been relaxed for the sake of historical interest.

In the assessment of unusual pieces without marks and with no documented provenance or information, the Antique Plate Committee plays an important role. This Committee, consisting of eight expert members of London's Goldsmiths' Hall, was established in 1939 to examine and adjudicate any piece of silver in order to determine its authenticity and to establish whether it is in contravention of the Hallmarking Act of 1973; they are bound to qualify their reasons should they declare a piece faked or altered (see Fakes & Alterations pp172–179).

## IMPORTED SILVER

The Customs Act of 1842 stipulated that all silver imported to Great Britain or Ireland was to be assayed and marked in a British assay office, a requirement to be back-dated 42 years, to 1800. This had the disastrous effect of subjecting Continental silver to being irrelevantly stamped with Queen Victoria's head. From 1904, all imported silver had to be marked with the relevant standard in decimal – for example, .925 for sterling silver, .958 for Britannia silver. The Hallmarking Act of 1973 dispensed with the decimal point and, whereas British silver of the Britannia standard is stamped 958.4 (parts per thousand), imported silver is still marked simply 958.

## DUTY DODGERS

With the imposition in Britain of the punitive tax on wrought plate from 1784–1890, there inevitably developed a number of methods of avoiding the duty. These methods of 'duty dodging', as it is referred to today, are seen as separate from the innocent alterations to silverwares which have occurred over the centuries, and from faking, carried out more recently to deliberately mislead the buying public (see Fakes and Alterations pp172 –179). Duty dodging had the sole purpose of avoiding paying the levy.

One such method involved the use of transposed hallmarks. A high quality silver piece was sent to assay; the stamped area was then removed and inserted into a piece of inferior quality. Hallmarks were also transposed from small pieces to much larger items, as the silver duty was partly based on weight.

The evidence of duty dodging is difficult to spot. One clue may be in the position of the marks, which tended to vary with fashion. For example, a Queen Anne coffee pot would usually be marked underneath the base, whereas an 18th-century coffee pot would tend to be stamped on the rim. A Queen Anne pot marked on the rim should therefore arouse suspicion.

The marks on early silver spoons, from c1680 to 1690, were randomly applied and it was not until c1700 that marks began to be arranged in groups. One famous silver faker made a cast of an original early spoon, including random marks, and made a set of six spoons from the mould. The identically positioned marks gave the forger away, and he was duly punished.

## ECCLESIASTICAL SILVER

Some of the finest early silver in Britain is to be found in churches. The manufacture and decoration of church plate has traditionally been of the highest standard of craftsmanship and has generally been well cared for. A certain standard of elaboration in decoration was maintained even during periods when the secular fashion was for simple, undecorated wares.

It is usually possible, with the compliance of the local church council, to gain access to some exquisite and historical silverwares – an interesting way to see some of the oldest and finest silver crafting around, and to study some genuine and ancient marks.

Church plate is of two types – that made specially for a church, which tends to represent faithfully the high style of the day, and that given to a church as a donation from a member of the congregation or a wealthy patron. The latter type is usually of domestic style bearing an inscription, naming the donor, the church and the date of the gift. Both types add significantly to our knowledge and understanding of the silver of any given period.

The requirements for a church service have evolved over centuries and typically consist of a chalice, ewers for the wine and water, a paten and the pyx. The number of other sacred vessels and decorative objects such as candlesticks, croziers and bells depends on the size and wealth of the particular church.

The Reformation, which began as a political shift away from the Roman Catholic church, had by the 16th century developed into a vengeful force. During the devastation which followed in its wake, ecclesiastical silverwares were sorted through, and all but the items essential for Communion confiscated. To avoid this desecration, many churches melted their silver down for coinage that could be hidden and used for other purposes. Ecclesiastical pre-Reformation silver is therefore rare. As rules governing worship were relaxed over the following centuries, the amount of church silver increased.

# ASSAY OFFICES

There are now only five Assay Offices remaining in Britain and Ireland. These are London, Birmingham, Sheffield, Edinburgh and Dublin. Birmingham Assay Office is now the largest – not only in Britain and Ireland, but in the entire world. In 2006, Birmingham Assay Office handled over 12 million items of precious metals.

All assay offices previously used punches to mark pieces and now, after extensive research, controlled lasers are used. Some items, such as rings, cannot be marked using a laser as they are too small and the curved edge makes the process difficult. Flat pieces, such as watch backs, are best suited for laser hallmarking.

From 1975, all the British assay offices, excluding Dublin, have an identical date letter system. This is shown below. Dublin Assay Office does not have the same date letter system as Britain, but it works in a similar way (see pp27–30).

| Year | Letter | Year | Letter |
|------|--------|------|--------|
| 1975 | A | 1993 | T |
| 1976 | B | 1994 | U |
| 1977 | C | 1995 | V |
| 1978 | D | 1996 | W |
| 1979 | E | 1997 | X |
| 1980 | F | 1998 | Y |
| 1981 | G | 1999 | Z |
| 1982 | H | 2000 | a |
| 1983 | I | 2001 | b |
| 1984 | K | 2002 | c |
| 1985 | L | 2003 | d |
| 1986 | M | 2004 | e |
| 1987 | N | 2005 | f |
| 1988 | O | 2006 | g |
| 1989 | P | 2007 | h |
| 1990 | Q | 2008 | i |
| 1991 | R | 2009 | j |
| 1992 | S | | |

# MAIN ASSAY OFFICES – ACTIVE

## LONDON

As early as 1180, an association of goldsmiths existed in London, although it was not legally recognized until Edward III's Act of 1327 (see Introduction pp6–14). This Act acknowledged the Worshipful Company of Goldsmiths, and gave them the right to enforce the assay laws. Until 1378, all silver had to be taken to Goldsmiths' Hall in the City of London for testing. Silver of the required quality was marked with the leopard's head. As other assay offices were granted powers of touch, this mark became associated with the London Assay Office. The leopard's head was surmounted by a crown between 1478 and 1821. Sometimes, between 1790 and 1820, especially on small articles, the mark was omitted altogether (see p12). The London goldsmiths are renowned for the very high standard of their work.

| | | | | | | | |
|---|---|---|---|---|---|---|---|
| 🦁👑 | | 1608 | 𝕷 | 1618 | 𝖆 | 1629 | 𝖒 |
| 1598 | 𝕬 | 1609 | 𝕸 | 1619 | 𝖇 | 1630 | 𝖓 |
| 1599 | 𝕭 | 1610 | 𝕹 | 1620 | 𝖈 | 1631 | 𝖔 |
| 1600 | 𝕮 | 1611 | 𝕺 | 1621 | 𝖉 | 1632 | 𝖕 |
| 1601 | 𝕯 | 1612 | 𝕻 | 1622 | 𝖊 | 1633 | 𝖖 |
| 1602 | 𝕰 | 1613 | 𝕼 | 1623 | 𝖋 | 1634 | 𝖗 |
| 1603 | 𝕱 | 1614 | 𝕽 | 1624 | 𝖌 | 1635 | 𝖘 |
| 1604 | 𝕲 | 1615 | 𝕾 | 1625 | 𝖍 | 1636 | 𝖙 |
| 1605 | 𝕳 | 1616 | 𝕿 | 1626 | 𝖎 | 1637 | 𝖛 |
| 1606 | 𝕴 | 1617 | 𝖁 | 1627 | 𝖏 | 🦁👑 | |
| 1607 | 𝕶 | 🦁👑 | | 1628 | 𝖑 | 1638 | 𝖆 |

| | | | |
|---|---|---|---|
| 1639 | 1667 | 1694 | 1722 |
| 1640 | 1668 | 1695 | 1723 |
| 1641 | 1669 | 1696 | 1724 |
| 1642 | 1670 | 1697 | 1725 |
| 1643 | 1671 | 1698 | 1726 |
| 1644 | 1672 | 1699 | 1727 |
| 1645 | 1673 | 1700 | 1728 |
| 1646 | 1674 | 1701 | 1729 |
| 1647 | 1675 | 1702 | 1730 |
| 1648 | 1676 | 1703 | 1731 |
| 1649 | 1677 | 1704 | 1732 |
| 1650 | 1678 | 1705 | 1733 |
| 1651 | 1679 | 1706 | 1734 |
| 1652 | 1680 | 1707 | 1735 |
| 1653 | 1681 | 1708 | 1736 |
| 1654 | 1682 | 1709 | 1737 |
| 1655 | 1683 | 1710 | 1738 |
| 1656 | 1684 | 1711 | 1739 |
| 1657 | 1685 | 1712 | 1740 |
| 1658 | 1686 | 1713 | 1741 |
| 1659 | 1687 | 1714 | 1742 |
| 1660 | 1688 | 1715 | 1743 |
| 1661 | 1689 | 1716 | 1744 |
| 1662 | 1690 | 1717 | 1745 |
| 1663 | 1691 | 1718 | 1746 |
| 1664 | 1692 | 1719 | 1747 |
| 1665 | 1693 | 1720 | 1748 |
| 1666 | | 1721 | |

**LONDON**

| Year | | Year | | Year | | Year | |
|---|---|---|---|---|---|---|---|
| 1749 | O | 1778 | C | 1806 | L | 1834 | t |
| 1750 | P | 1779 | d | 1807 | M | 1835 | u |
| 1751 | q | 1780 | e | 1808 | N | 1836 | A |
| 1752 | r | 1781 | f | 1809 | O | 1837 | B |
| 1753 | s | 1782 | g | 1810 | P | | [marks] |
| 1754 | t | 1783 | h | 1811 | Q | 1838 | C |
| 1755 | U | | [marks] | 1812 | R | 1839 | D |
| | [marks] | 1784 | i | 1813 | S | 1840 | E |
| 1756 | A | 1785 | k | 1814 | T | 1841 | F |
| 1757 | B | | [marks] | 1815 | U | 1842 | G |
| 1758 | C | 1786 | l | 1816 | a | 1843 | H |
| 1759 | D | 1787 | m | 1817 | b | 1844 | J |
| 1760 | E | 1788 | n | 1818 | C | 1845 | K |
| 1761 | F | 1789 | O | 1819 | d | 1846 | L |
| 1762 | G | 1790 | P | 1820 | e | 1847 | M |
| 1763 | H | 1791 | q | 1821 | f | 1848 | N |
| 1764 | J | 1792 | r | | [marks] | 1849 | O |
| 1765 | h | 1793 | S | 1822 | g | 1850 | P |
| 1766 | J | 1794 | t | 1823 | h | 1851 | Q |
| 1767 | m | 1795 | u | 1824 | i | 1852 | R |
| 1768 | n | 1796 | A | 1825 | k | 1853 | S |
| 1769 | O | 1797 | B | 1826 | l | 1854 | T |
| 1770 | P | 1798 | C | 1827 | m | 1855 | U |
| 1771 | Q | 1799 | D | 1828 | n | 1856 | a |
| 1772 | R | 1800 | E | 1829 | o | 1857 | b |
| 1773 | S | 1801 | F | 1830 | p | 1858 | c |
| 1774 | T | 1802 | G | 1831 | q | 1859 | d |
| 1775 | U | 1803 | H | 1832 | r | 1860 | e |
| 1776 | a | 1804 | I | 1833 | s | 1861 | f |
| 1777 | b | 1805 | K | | [marks] | 1862 | g |

| Year | Letter | Year | Letter | Year | Letter | Year | Letter |
|---|---|---|---|---|---|---|---|
| 1863 | ḣ | 1892 | Ⓡ | 1920 | ⓔ | 1948 | N |
| 1864 | i | 1893 | Ⓢ | 1921 | f | 1949 | O |
| 1865 | k | 1894 | Ⓣ | 1922 | g | 1950 | P |
| 1866 | l | 1895 | Ⓤ | ☒ ☒ | | 1951 | Q |
| 1867 | m | ☒ ☒ | | 1923 | h | 1952 | R |
| 1868 | n | 1896 | a | 1924 | i | 1953 | S |
| 1869 | o | 1897 | b | 1925 | k | 1954 | T |
| 1870 | p | 1898 | c | 1926 | l | 1955 | U |
| 1871 | q | 1899 | d | 1927 | m | 1956 | a |
| 1872 | r | 1900 | e | 1928 | n | 1957 | b |
| 1873 | ŝ | 1901 | f | 1929 | o | 1958 | c |
| 1874 | t | 1902 | g | 1930 | p | 1959 | d |
| 1875 | u | 1903 | h | 1931 | q | 1960 | e |
| 1876 | A | 1904 | i | 1932 | r | 1961 | f |
| 1877 | B | 1905 | k | 1933 | s | 1962 | g |
| 1878 | C | 1906 | l | 1934 | t | 1963 | h |
| 1879 | D | 1907 | m | 1935 | u | 1964 | i |
| 1880 | E | 1908 | n | ☒ ☒ | | 1965 | k |
| 1881 | F | 1909 | O | 1936 | A | 1966 | l |
| 1882 | G | 1910 | P | 1937 | B | 1967 | m |
| 1883 | H | 1911 | q | 1938 | C | 1968 | n |
| 1884 | I | 1912 | r | 1939 | D | 1969 | o |
| 1885 | K | 1913 | s | 1940 | E | 1970 | p |
| 1886 | L | 1914 | t | 1941 | F | 1971 | q |
| 1887 | M | 1915 | u | 1942 | G | 1972 | r |
| 1888 | N | ☒ ☒ | | 1943 | H | 1973 | s |
| 1889 | O | 1916 | a | 1944 | I | 1974 | t |
| 1890 | P | 1917 | b | 1945 | K | ☒ ☒ | |
| ☒ ☒ | | 1918 | c | 1946 | L | | |
| 1891 | Q | 1919 | d | 1947 | M | | |

## EDINBURGH

Silverwares bearing Scottish hallmarks survive from
the mid-16th century. The silver standard had been
established in Scotland in 1457, by James II of Scotland.
Scotland was not subject to the Britannia Standard,
but when sterling was restored in England in 1720,
the standard of silver was raised in Scotland to the same
level of purity and sixpence an ounce tax was also levied.
The Edinburgh mark can be found on an extensive range
of domestic and ecclesiastical plate.

| Year | Mark | Year | Mark | Year | Mark | Year | Mark |
|---|---|---|---|---|---|---|---|
| 1609 | | | | 1700 | | 1722 | |
| 1611 | | 1681 | | 1701 | | 1723 | |
| 1617–19 | | | | 1702 | | 1724 | |
| 1617 | | 1682 | | 1703 | | 1725 | |
| 1613–21 | | 1683 | | 1704 | | 1726 | |
| 1616 | | 1684 | | 1705 | | 1727 | |
| 1633 | | 1685 | | 1706 | | 1728 | |
| 1637 | | 1686 | | 1707 | | 1729 | |
| 1640 | | 1687 | | 1708 | | 1730 | |
| 1642 | | 1688 | | 1709 | | 1731 | |
| 1643 | | 1689 | | 1710 | | 1732 | |
| 1644 | | 1690 | | 1711 | | 1733 | |
| 1649-57 | | 1691 | | 1712 | | 1734 | |
| 1651-9 | | 1692 | | 1713 | | 1735 | |
| 1660 | | 1693 | | 1714 | | 1736 | |
| 1663-81 | | 1694 | | 1715 | | 1737 | |
| 1665 | | 1695 | | 1716 | | 1738 | |
| 1669-75 | | 1696 | | 1717 | | 1739 | |
| 1675-7 | | 1697 | | 1718 | | 1740 | |
| | | 1698 | | 1719 | | 1741 | |
| | | 1699 | | 1720 | | 1742 | |
| | | | | 1721 | | 1743 | |
| | | | | | | 1744 | |

| Year | Mark | Year | Mark | Year | Mark | Year | Mark |
| --- | --- | --- | --- | --- | --- | --- | --- |
| 1745 | Q | 1774 | U | 1802 | W | 1831 | Z |
| 1746 | R | 1775 | V | 1803 | X | 1832 | A |
| 1747 | S | 1776 | W | 1804 | Y | 1833 | B |
| 1748 | T | 1777 | X | 1805 | Z | 1834 | C |
| 1749 | U | 1778 | Y | 1806 | a | 1835 | D |
| 1750 | V | 1779 | Z | 1807 | b | 1836 | E |
| 1751 | W | 1780 | A | 1808 | C | 1837 | F |
| 1752 | X | 1781 | B | 1809 | d | 1838 | G |
| 1753 | Y | 1782 | C | 1810 | e | 1839 | H |
| 1754 | Z | 1783 | D | 1811 | f | 1840 | J |
| 1755 | A | | [castle] [thistle] [sovereign's head] | 1812 | g | | [castle] [thistle] [sovereign's head] |
| 1756 | B | 1784 | E | 1813 | h | 1841 | K |
| 1757 | C | 1785 | F | 1814 | i | 1842 | L |
| 1758 | D | | [castle] [thistle] [sovereign's head] | 1815 | j | 1843 | M |
| | [castle] [thistle] | 1786 | G | 1816 | k | 1844 | N |
| 1759 | E | 1787 | G | 1817 | l | 1845 | O |
| 1760 | F | 1788 | H | 1818 | m | 1846 | P |
| 1761 | G | 1789 | JJ | 1819 | n | 1847 | Q |
| 1762 | H | 1790 | K | | [castle] [thistle] [sovereign's head] | 1848 | R |
| 1763 | I | 1791 | L | 1820 | O | 1849 | S |
| 1764 | K | 1792 | M | 1821 | P | 1850 | T |
| 1765 | L | 1793 | N | 1822 | q | 1851 | U |
| 1766 | M | 1794 | O | 1823 | r | 1852 | V |
| 1767 | N | 1795 | P | 1824 | s | 1853 | W |
| 1768 | O | 1796 | Q | 1825 | t | 1854 | X |
| 1769 | P | 1797 | R | 1826 | u | 1855 | Y |
| 1770 | Q | 1798 | S | 1827 | v | 1856 | Z |
| 1771 | R | 1799 | T | 1828 | w | 1857 | A |
| 1772 | S | 1800 | U | 1829 | x | 1858 | B |
| 1773 | T | 1801 | V | 1830 | y | 1859 | C |

**EDINBURGH**

| Year | Mark | Year | Mark | Year | Mark | Year | Mark |
|------|------|------|------|------|------|------|------|
| 1860 | Ⓓ | 1890 | ⓘ | 1919 | Ⓞ | 1949 | 𝕵 |
| 1861 | Ⓔ | | 🛡 🛡 | 1920 | Ⓟ | 1950 | 𝕶 |
| 1862 | Ⓕ | 1891 | ⓚ | 1921 | Ⓠ | 1951 | 𝕷 |
| 1863 | Ⓖ | 1892 | ⓛ | 1922 | Ⓡ | 1952 | 𝕸 |
| 1864 | Ⓗ | 1893 | ⓜ | 1923 | Ⓢ | 1953 | 𝕹 |
| 1865 | Ⓘ | 1894 | ⓝ | 1924 | Ⓣ | 1954 | 𝕺 |
| 1866 | Ⓚ | 1895 | ⓞ | 1925 | Ⓤ | 1955 | 𝕻 |
| 1867 | Ⓛ | 1896 | ⓟ | 1926 | Ⓥ | 1956 | 𝕬 |
| 1868 | Ⓜ | 1897 | ⓠ | 1927 | Ⓦ | 1957 | 𝕭 |
| 1869 | Ⓝ | 1898 | ⓡ | 1928 | Ⓧ | 1958 | 𝕮 |
| 1870 | Ⓞ | 1899 | ⓢ | 1929 | Ⓨ | 1959 | 𝕯 |
| 1871 | Ⓟ | 1900 | ⓣ | 1930 | Ⓩ | 1960 | 𝕰 |
| 1872 | Ⓠ | 1901 | ⓤ | 1931 | 𝒜 | 1961 | 𝕱 |
| 1873 | Ⓡ | 1902 | ⓦ | 1932 | 𝐵 | 1962 | 𝕲 |
| 1874 | Ⓢ | 1903 | ⓧ | 1933 | 𝒞 | 1963 | 𝕳 |
| 1875 | Ⓣ | 1904 | ⓨ | 1934 | 𝒟 | 1964 | 𝕴 |
| 1876 | Ⓤ | 1905 | ⓩ | 1935 | 𝐸 | 1965 | 𝕶 |
| 1877 | Ⓥ | 1906 | Ⓐ | 1936 | 𝐹 | 1966 | 𝕷 |
| 1878 | Ⓦ | 1907 | Ⓑ | 1937 | 𝒢 | 1967 | 𝕸 |
| 1879 | Ⓧ | 1908 | Ⓒ | 1938 | 𝐻 | 1968 | 𝕹 |
| 1880 | Ⓨ | 1909 | Ⓓ | 1939 | 𝐼 | 1969 | 𝕺 |
| 1881 | Ⓩ | 1910 | Ⓔ | 1940 | 𝒦 | 1970 | 𝕻 |
| 1882 | ⓐ | 1911 | Ⓕ | 1941 | 𝒵 | 1971 | 𝕼 |
| 1883 | ⓑ | 1912 | Ⓖ | 1942 | 𝐿 | 1972 | 𝕽 |
| 1884 | ⓒ | 1913 | Ⓗ | 1943 | 𝒩 | 1973 | 𝕾 |
| 1885 | ⓓ | 1914 | Ⓘ | 1944 | 𝒪 | 1974 | 𝕾 |
| 1886 | ⓔ | 1915 | Ⓚ | 1945 | 𝒫 | | 🛡 🦁 |
| 1887 | ⓕ | 1916 | Ⓛ | 1946 | 𝒬 | | |
| 1888 | ⓖ | 1917 | Ⓜ | 1947 | 𝑅 | | |
| 1889 | ⓗ | 1918 | Ⓝ | 1948 | 𝒮 | | |

## BIRMINGHAM

The Birmingham office began assaying in 1773, having been convened by an Act of Parliament in 1772. Birmingham's mark shows an upright anchor and is usually accompanied by a lion passant, a date letter and a duty mark (the sovereign's head), and the maker's initials. Birmingham marks are often seen on smallwares, such as vinaigrettes, snuff-boxes and buckles.

| | | | | | | | |
|---|---|---|---|---|---|---|---|
| | | 1794 | W | 1818 | u | 1840 | ℛ |
| 1773 | A | 1795 | X | 1819 | V | 1841 | s |
| 1774 | B | 1796 | Y | 1820 | W | 1842 | T |
| 1775 | C | 1797 | Z | 1821 | X | 1843 | U |
| 1776 | D | 1798 | a | 1822 | y | 1844 | V |
| 1777 | E | 1799 | b | 1823 | Z | 1845 | W |
| 1778 | F | 1800 | c | 1824 | a | 1846 | X |
| 1779 | G | 1801 | d | 1825 | B | 1847 | Y |
| 1780 | H | 1802 | e | 1826 | C | 1848 | Z |
| 1781 | I | 1803 | f | 1827 | D | 1849 | A |
| 1782 | K | 1804 | g | 1828 | E | 1850 | B |
| 1783 | L | 1805 | h | 1829 | F | 1851 | C |
| 1784 | M | 1806 | i | 1830 | G | 1852 | D |
| 1785 | N | 1807 | J | 1831 | H | 1853 | E |
| 1786 | O | 1808 | k | 1832 | J | 1854 | F |
| 1787 | P | 1809 | l | 1833 | K | 1855 | G |
| 1788 | Q | 1810 | m | 1834 | L | 1856 | H |
| 1789 | R | 1811 | n | 1835 | M | 1857 | I |
| 1790 | S | 1812 | o | 1836 | N | 1858 | J |
| 1791 | T | 1813 | p | 1837 | O | 1859 | K |
| 1792 | U | 1814 | q | 1838 | P | 1860 | L |
| 1793 | V | 1815 | r | 1839 | Q | 1861 | M |
| | | 1816 | s | | | 1862 | N |
| | | 1817 | t | | | | |

| Year | Mark | Year | Mark | Year | Mark | Year | Mark |
|------|------|------|------|------|------|------|------|
| 1863 | O | 1891 | r | 1920 | v | | |
| 1864 | P | 1892 | s | 1921 | w | 1950 | A |
| 1865 | Q | 1893 | t | 1922 | x | 1951 | B |
| 1866 | R | 1894 | u | 1923 | y | 1952 | C |
| 1867 | S | 1895 | v | 1924 | z | 1953 | D |
| 1868 | T | 1896 | w | 1925 | A | 1954 | E |
| 1869 | U | 1897 | x | 1926 | B | 1955 | F |
| 1870 | V | 1898 | y | 1927 | C | 1956 | G |
| 1871 | W | 1899 | z | 1928 | D | 1957 | H |
| 1872 | X | | ⚓ 🦁 | 1929 | E | 1958 | J |
| 1873 | Y | 1900 | a | 1930 | F | 1959 | K |
| 1874 | Z | 1901 | b | 1931 | G | 1960 | L |
| 🐘 ⚓ 👑 | | 1902 | c | 1932 | H | 1961 | M |
| 1875 | a | 1903 | d | 1933 | J | 1962 | N |
| 1876 | b | 1904 | e | 1934 | K | 1963 | O |
| 1877 | c | 1905 | f | 1935 | L | 1964 | P |
| 1878 | d | 1906 | g | 1936 | M | 1965 | Q |
| 1879 | e | 1907 | h | 1937 | N | 1966 | R |
| 1880 | f | 1908 | i | 1938 | O | 1967 | S |
| 1881 | g | 1909 | k | 1939 | P | 1968 | T |
| 1882 | h | 1910 | l | 1940 | Q | 1969 | U |
| 1883 | i | 1911 | m | 1941 | R | 1970 | V |
| 1884 | k | 1912 | n | 1942 | S | 1971 | W |
| 1885 | l | 1913 | o | 1943 | T | 1972 | X |
| 1886 | m | 1914 | p | 1944 | U | ⚓ 🦁 | |
| 1887 | n | 1915 | q | 1945 | V | 1973 | Y |
| 1888 | o | 1916 | r | 1946 | W | ⚓ 🦁 | |
| 1889 | p | 1917 | s | 1947 | X | 1974 | Z |
| 1890 | q | 1918 | t | 1948 | Y | ⚓ 🦁 | |
| 🦁 ⚓ | | 1919 | u | 1949 | Z | | |

# SHEFFIELD

By the middle of the 18th century, Sheffield was a major manufacturing centre for silver. The efforts of Matthew Boulton, a Birmingham industrialist, led to the Act of Parliament in which Sheffield was established as an assay office in 1773. Until 1974, Sheffield's mark depicted a crown which featured along with the usual marks used at other assay offices. Date letters were first used in 1773, starting with E, and changed irregularly each year until 1824. After this date they were arranged in alphabetical order. The region was renowned for candlesticks.

| | | | | | | | |
|---|---|---|---|---|---|---|---|
| | 🦁👑 | 1793 | q | 1816 | T | 1838 | S |
| 1773 | E | 1794 | m | 1817 | X | 1839 | t |
| 1774 | F | 1795 | q | 1818 | I | | 🦁👑🛡 |
| 1775 | H | 1796 | Z | 1819 | V | 1840 | u |
| 1776 | R | 1797 | X | 1820 | Q | 1841 | V |
| 1777 | h | 1798 | V | 1821 | Y | 1842 | X |
| 1778 | S | 1799 | E | 1822 | Z | 1843 | Z |
| 1779 | A | 1800 | N | 1823 | U | 1844 | A |
| 1780 | C | 1801 | H | 1824 | a | 1845 | B |
| 1781 | D | 1802 | M | 1825 | b | 1846 | C |
| 1782 | G | 1803 | F | 1826 | C | 1847 | D |
| 1783 | B | 1804 | G | 1827 | d | 1848 | E |
| | 🦁👑🛡 | 1805 | B | 1828 | e | 1849 | F |
| 1784 | J | 1806 | A | 1829 | f | 1850 | G |
| 1785 | V | 1807 | S | 1830 | g | 1851 | H |
| | 🦁👑🛡 | 1808 | P | 1831 | h | 1852 | I |
| 1786 | k | 1809 | K | 1832 | k | 1853 | K |
| 1787 | J | 1810 | L | 1833 | l | 1854 | L |
| 1788 | m | 1811 | C | | 🦁👑🛡 | 1855 | M |
| 1789 | m | 1812 | D | 1834 | m | 1856 | N |
| 1790 | L | 1813 | R | 1835 | P | 1857 | O |
| 1791 | P | 1814 | W | 1836 | q | 1858 | P |
| 1792 | u | 1815 | O | 1837 | r | 1859 | R |

**SHEFFIELD**

| Year | Mark | Year | Mark | Year | Mark | Year | Mark |
|------|------|------|------|------|------|------|------|
| 1860 | S | 1889 | W | 1917 | ʒ | 1946 | D |
| 1861 | T | 1890 | X | | 👑 🦁 | 1947 | E |
| 1862 | U | | 👑 🦁 | 1918 | a | 1948 | F |
| 1863 | V | 1891 | Y | 1919 | b | 1949 | G |
| 1864 | W | 1892 | Z | 1920 | c | 1950 | H |
| 1865 | X | 1893 | a | 1921 | d | 1951 | I |
| 1866 | Y | 1894 | b | 1922 | e | 1952 | K |
| 1867 | Z | 1895 | c | 1923 | f | 1953 | L |
| | 👑 🦁 🌐 | 1896 | d | 1924 | g | 1954 | M |
| 1868 | A | 1897 | e | 1925 | h | 1955 | N |
| 1869 | B | 1898 | f | 1926 | i | 1956 | O |
| 1870 | C | 1899 | g | 1927 | k | 1957 | P |
| 1871 | D | 1900 | h | 1928 | l | 1958 | Q |
| 1872 | E | 1901 | i | 1929 | m | 1959 | R |
| 1873 | F | 1902 | k | 1930 | n | 1960 | S |
| 1874 | G | 1903 | l | 1931 | o | 1961 | T |
| 1875 | H | 1904 | m | 1932 | p | 1962 | U |
| 1876 | J | 1905 | n | 1933 | q | 1963 | V |
| 1877 | K | 1906 | o | 1934 | r | 1964 | W |
| 1878 | L | 1907 | p | 1935 | s | 1965 | X |
| 1879 | M | 1908 | q | 1936 | t | 1966 | Y |
| 1880 | N | 1909 | r | 1937 | u | 1967 | Z |
| 1881 | O | 1910 | s | 1938 | v | 1968 | A |
| 1882 | P | 1911 | t | 1939 | w | 1969 | B |
| 1883 | Q | 1912 | u | 1940 | x | 1970 | C |
| 1884 | R | 1913 | v | 1941 | y | 1971 | D |
| 1885 | S | | 👑 🦁 | 1942 | z | 1972 | E |
| 1886 | T | 1914 | w | 1943 | A | 1973 | F |
| 1887 | U | 1915 | x | 1944 | B | 1974 | G |
| 1888 | V | 1916 | y | 1945 | C | | 🔲 🦁 |

## DUBLIN

Although Dublin's city council decreed that silver of the correct standard (coin) was to be marked with a lion, a harp and a castle, Irish silver was only sporadically marked. In 1637 a crowned harp with a date letter was introduced, with a maker's mark system being introduced in 1638; marked examples survive from that date onwards. In 1731 the figure of Hibernia was introduced, and in 1807 the monarch's head was added as the duty mark, giving Dublin five marks until 1890, when the monarch's head was again dropped. The Dublin mark is found on a wide variety of silver wares, and Irish workmanship is acclaimed for its excellent decorative style. After the Revocation of the Edict of Nantes in 1685, many Huguenot goldsmiths emigrated to Dublin, bringing Continental influences to Irish silver which lasted throughout much of the 18th century.

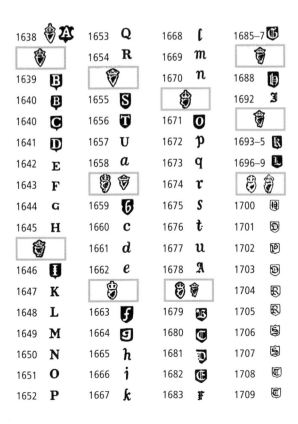

| 1638 | 🛡️🅐 | 1653 | Q | 1668 | l | 1685–7 | 🛡️ |
| | 🛡️ | 1654 | R | 1669 | m | | 🛡️ |
| 1639 | B | | 🛡️ | 1670 | n | 1688 | 🛡️ |
| 1640 | B | 1655 | S | | 🛡️ | 1692 | J |
| 1640 | C | 1656 | T | 1671 | O | | 🛡️ |
| 1641 | D | 1657 | U | 1672 | p | 1693–5 | 🛡️ |
| 1642 | E | 1658 | a | 1673 | q | 1696–9 | 🛡️ |
| 1643 | F | | 🛡️ 🛡️ | 1674 | r | | 🛡️ 🛡️ |
| 1644 | G | 1659 | b | 1675 | s | 1700 | 🛡️ |
| 1645 | H | 1660 | c | 1676 | t | 1701 | 🛡️ |
| | 🛡️ | 1661 | d | 1677 | u | 1702 | 🛡️ |
| 1646 | I | 1662 | e | 1678 | A | 1703 | 🛡️ |
| 1647 | K | | 🛡️ | | 🛡️ 🛡️ | 1704 | 🛡️ |
| 1648 | L | 1663 | f | 1679 | 🛡️ | 1705 | 🛡️ |
| 1649 | M | 1664 | g | 1680 | 🛡️ | 1706 | 🛡️ |
| 1650 | N | 1665 | h | 1681 | 🛡️ | 1707 | 🛡️ |
| 1651 | O | 1666 | i | 1682 | 🛡️ | 1708 | 🛡️ |
| 1652 | P | 1667 | k | 1683 | F | 1709 | 🛡️ |

**DUBLIN**

| | | | |
|---|---|---|---|
| 1710 | 1737 | 1765 | 1792 |
| 1711 | 1738 | 1766 | |
| 1712 | 1739 | 1767 | 1793 |
| 1713 | 1740 | 1768 | 1794 |
| 1714 | 1741 | 1769 | 1795 |
| 1715 | | 1770 | 1796 |
| 1716 | 1741 | 1771 | |
| | 1742 | 1772 | 1797 |
| 1717 | 1743 | | 1798 |
| 1718 | 1744 | 1773 | 1799 |
| 1719 | 1745 | 1774 | 1800 |
| | 1746 | 1775 | 1801 |
| 1720 | | | 1802 |
| 1721 | 1747 | 1776 | 1803 |
| 1722 | 1748 | 1777 | 1804 |
| 1723 | 1749 | 1778 | 1805 |
| 1724 | 1750 | 1779 | 1806 |
| 1725 | 1751 | 1780 | 1807 |
| 1726 | 1752 | 1781 | 1808 |
| 1727 | 1753 | 1782 | 1809 |
| 1728 | 1754 | 1783 | |
| 1729 | 1755 | 1784 | 1810 |
| 1730 | 1757 | 1785 | 1811 |
| | 1758 | 1786 | 1812 |
| 1731 | 1759 | | 1813 |
| 1732 | | 1787 | 1814 |
| 1733 | 1760 | 1788 | 1815 |
| 1734 | 1761 | 1789 | 1816 |
| 1735 | 1762 | 1790 | 1817 |
| 1736 | 1763 | 1791 | 1818 |
| | 1764 | | |

| Year | Mark | Year | Mark | Year | Mark | Year | Mark |
|------|------|------|------|------|------|------|------|
| 1819 | Y | 1839 | T | — | 🛡🛡🛡 | 1892 | W |
| 1820 | Z | 1840 | U | 1864 | t | 1893 | X |
| — | 🛡🛡🛡 | 1841 | V | 1865 | u | 1894 | V |
| 1821 | A | — | 🛡🛡 | 1866 | v | 1895 | Z |
| 1822 | B C | 1842 | W | 1867 | w | — | 🛡🛡 |
| 1823 | C | 1843 | X | 1868 | X | 1896 | A |
| 1824 | D | — | 🛡🛡 | 1869 | Y | 1897 | B |
| 1825 | E e | 1844 | Y | 1870 | Z | 1898 | C |
| 1826 | F | — | 🛡🛡 | — | 🛡🛡🛡 | 1899 | D |
| — | 🛡🛡🛡 | 1845 | Z | 1871 | A | 1900 | E |
| 1827 | G | — | 🛡🛡🛡 | 1872 | B | 1901 | F |
| — | 🛡🛡🛡 | 1846 | a | 1873 | C | 1902 | G |
| 1828 | H | 1847 | b | 1874 | D | 1903 | H |
| — | 🛡🛡🛡 | 1848 | C | 1875 | E | 1904 | I |
| 1829 | I | 1849 | d | 1876 | F | 1905 | K |
| — | 🛡🛡🛡 | 1850 | e | 1877 | G | 1906 | L |
| 1830 | K | 1851 | f f | 1878 | H | 1907 | M |
| — | 🛡🛡🛡 | 1852 | g g | 1879 | U | 1908 | N |
| 1831 | L | 1853 | h h | 1880 | K | 1909 | O |
| 1832 | M | 1854 | J | 1881 | L | 1910 | P |
| — | 🛡🛡 | — | 🛡🛡🛡 | 1882 | M | 1911 | Q |
| 1833 | N | 1855 | k | 1883 | N | 1912 | R |
| — | 🛡🛡🛡 | 1856 | l | 1884 | O | 1913 | S |
| 1834 | O | 1857 | m | 1885 | P | 1914 | T |
| 1835 | P | 1858 | n | 1886 | Q | 1915 | U |
| 1836 | Q | 1859 | O | 1887 | R | — | 🛡🛡 |
| — | 🛡🛡🛡 | 1860 | P | 1888 | S | 1916 | A |
| 1837 | R | 1861 | Q | 1889 | T | 1917 | b |
| 1838 | S | 1862 | T | 1890 | U | 1918 | C |
| — | 🛡🛡 | 1863 | S | 1891 | V | 1919 | D |

**DUBLIN**

| Year | | Year | | Year | | Year | |
|---|---|---|---|---|---|---|---|
| 1920 | 🔤 | | | |  | 1986 | 𝐴 |
| 1921 | 🔤 | 1942 | A | 1966 | Y | | |
| 1922 | 🔤 | 1943 | B | | | 1987 | 𝐵 |
| 1923 | 🔤 | 1944 | C | 1967 | Z | | |
| 1924 | 🔤 | 1945 | D | | | 1988 | 𝐶 |
| 1925 | 🔤 | 1946 | E | 1968 | a | | |
| 1926 | 🔤 | 1947 | F | 1969 | b | 1989 | 𝐷 |
| 1927 | 🔤 | 1948 | G | 1970 | c | 1990 | 𝐸 |
| 1928 | 🔤 | 1949 | H | 1971 | ð | 1991 | 𝐹 |
| 1929 | 🔤 | 1950 | I | 1972 | e | 1992 | 𝐺 |
| 1930 | 🔤 | 1951 | J | | | 1993 | 𝐻 |
| | | 1952 | K | 1973 | F | 1994 | 𝐼 |
| | | 1953 | L | | | 1995 | 𝐽 |
| | | 1954 | M | 1974 | s | 1996 | 𝐾 |
| | | | | 1975 | h | 1997 | 𝐿 |
| | | 1955 | N | 1976 | i | 1998 | 𝑀 |
| | | 1956 | O | 1977 | l | | |
| 1932 | 🔤 | 1957 | P | 1978 | m | 1999 | 𝑁 |
| 1933 | 🔤 | 1958 | Q | 1979 | n | 2000 | 𝑂 |
| 1934 | 🔤 | 1959 | R | 1980 | o | | |
| 1935 | 🔤 | 1960 | S | | | 2001 | 𝑄 |
| 1936 | 🔤 | 1961 | T | 1981 | p | | |
| 1937 | 🔤 | 1962 | U | 1982 | R | 2002 | 𝑅 |
| 1938 | 🔤 | 1963 | V | 1983 | s | 2003 | 𝑆 |
| 1939 | 🔤 | 1964 | W | 1984 | c | 2004 | 𝑇 |
| 1940 | 🔤 | 1965 | X | 1985 | U | 2005 | 𝑈 |
| 1941 | 🔤 | | | | | | |

Up to 1931 the date letter was changed on 1st June. The Q of 1932 began on 1st January

# MAIN ASSAY OFFICES – INACTIVE

## EXETER

The earliest Exeter assay mark dates back to the mid-16thC and consists of the letter X, usually in a round shield with a crown on top. Assay marking in Exeter was erratic until c1700, and although many craftsmen worked in the region, little surviving silver bears the mark. After 1700, the marks are found on ecclesiastic and domestic wares. It closed 1883.

| Year | Mark | Year | Mark | Year | Mark | Year | Mark |
|------|------|------|------|------|------|------|------|
| 1600 | ⬡ | 1676 | ⬡ | 1714 | O | 1737 | n |
| 1600 | ⬡ | 1676 | ⬡ | 1715 | P | 1738 | o |
| c1600 | ⬡ | 1680 | ⬡ ⬡ | 1716 | Q | 1739 | p |
| 1606 | ⬡ | 1680 | ⬡ | 1717 | R | 1740 | q |
| | ⬡ | 1690 | EX ON | 1718 | S | 1741 | r |
| 1610 | a | 1690 | ⬡ | 1719 | T | 1742 | s |
| 1620 | b | 1690 | ⬡ | 1720 | V | 1743 | t |
| 1620 | ⬡ | 1690 | ⬡ ⬡ ⬡ | 1721 | W | 1744 | u |
| 1620 | ⬡ ⬡ | 1690 | ⬡ ⬡ | 1722 | X | 1745 | w |
| c1630 | ⬡ | 1698 | X ⬡ | 1723 | Y | 1746 | v |
| c1630 | ⬡ ⬡ | 1701 | A | 1724 | Z | 1747 | y |
| c1635 | ⬡ | 1702 | B | 1725 | a | 1748 | z |
| c1635 | ⬡ | 1703 | C | 1726 | h | 1749 | A |
| 1635 | ⬡ | 1703 | C | 1727 | c | 1750 | B |
| 1640 | ⬡ ⬡ a | 1704 | D | 1728 | d | 1751 | C |
| 1640 | ⬡ | 1705 | E | 1729 | e | 1752 | D |
| 1640 | ⬡ | 1706 | F | 1730 | f | 1753 | E |
| 1640 | ⬡ | 1707 | G | 1731 | g | 1754 | F |
| 1640 | ⬡ | 1708 | H | 1732 | h | 1755 | G |
| 1640–50 | ⬡ ⬡ | 1709 | I | 1733 | u | 1756 | H |
| 1640–50 | ⬡ | 1710 | K | 1734 | K | 1757 | I |
| 1640–50 | ⬡ | 1711 | L | 1735 | I | 1758 | K |
| 1640–50 | ⬡ | 1712 | M | 1736 | m | 1759 | L |
| 1646–98 | ⬡ | 1713 | N | | | 1760 | M |
| 1670 | X | | | | | | |

**EXETER**

| Year | Mark | Year | Mark | Year | Mark | Year | Mark |
|---|---|---|---|---|---|---|---|
| 1761 | N | 1788 | P | 1815 | T | | (three marks) |
| 1762 | O | 1789 | Q | 1816 | U | 1841 | e |
| 1763 | P | 1790 | R | | (three marks) | 1842 | f |
| 1764 | Q | 1791 | S | 1817 | a | | (three marks) |
| 1765 | R | 1792 | T | 1818 | b | 1843 | g |
| 1766 | S | 1793 | U | 1819 | c | 1844 | h |
| 1767 | T | 1794 | W | 1820 | d | 1845 | i |
| 1768 | U | 1795 | X | 1821 | e | 1846 | k |
| 1769 | W | 1796 | Y | 1822 | f (two marks) | 1847 | l |
| 1770 | X | | (three marks) | 1823 | g | 1848 | m |
| 1771 | Y | 1797 | A | 1824 | h | 1849 | n |
| 1772 | Z | 1798 | B | 1825 | i | 1850 | o |
| | (three marks) | 1799 | C (two marks) | 1826 | k | 1851 | p |
| 1773 | A | 1800 | D | 1827 | l | 1852 | q |
| 1774 | B | 1801 | E | 1828 | m | 1853 | r |
| 1775 | C | 1802 | F | 1829 | n | 1854 | s |
| 1776 | D | 1803 | G | 1830 | o | 1855 | t |
| 1777 | E | 1804 | H | | (three marks) | 1856 | u |
| Leopard's head was not used after 1777 | | | (three marks) | 1831 | p | | (three marks) |
| | | 1805 | I | 1832 | q | 1857 | A |
| 1778 | F | 1806 | K | | (three marks) | 1858 | B |
| 1779 | G | 1807 | L | 1833 | r | 1859 | C |
| 1780 | H | 1808 | M | 1834 | s (two marks) | 1860 | D |
| 1781 | I | 1809 | N | 1835 | t | 1861 | E |
| 1782 | J | 1810 | O | 1836 | u | 1862 | F |
| 1783 | K | 1811 | P | | (three marks) | 1863 | G |
| 1784 | L (two marks) | 1812 | Q | 1837 | A (two marks) | 1864 | H |
| 1785 | M | 1813 | R | 1838 | B (two marks) | 1865 | I |
| 1786 | N (two marks) | 1814 | S | 1839 | C | 1866 | K |
| 1787 | O | 1815 | T | 1840 | D | 1867 | L |

| | | | | | | | |
|---|---|---|---|---|---|---|---|
| 1868 | M | 1872 | Q | 1876 | U | 1879 | C |
| 1869 | N | 1873 | R | | | 1880 | D |
| 1870 | O | 1874 | S | 1877 | A | 1881 | E |
| 1871 | P | 1875 | T | 1878 | B | 1882 | F |

## NORWICH

There were at least a dozen silversmiths active in Norwich as early as the 13th century. Norwich was granted power of assay by Henry VI's statute of 1423. The original mark showed a castle surmounting a lion passant, and wares were also stamped with the date letter and maker's mark. In the first part of the 17th century a mark depicting a crowned seeded rose was introduced, to be replaced in the last half of the century by a stemmed rose. Assaying of silver in Norwich was sporadic and probably ceased altogether after 1701. From remaining examples it seems that the city specialized in church plate and spoons of a high standard.

YORK

## YORK

York was granted power of assay by Henry VI's statute of 1423, but there is evidence of the existence of a local touch from as early as 1410. The original mark was a half leopard's head with a fleur-de-lys joined together in one shield, followed with a sequence of date letters and makers' marks. The leopard's head was replaced by a half-seeded rose by the end of the 17th century, and in 1701 it was changed to five lions passant on a cross.

| | | | |
|---|---|---|---|
| 1607 | 1627 | 1649 | 1669 |
| 1608 | 1628 | 1650 | 1670 |
| 1609 | 1629 | 1651 | 1671 |
| 1610 | 1630 | 1652 | |
| 1611 | 1631 | 1653 | 1672 |
| 1612 | | 1654 | 1673 |
| 1613 | 1632 | 1655 | 1674 |
| 1614 | 1633 | 1656 | 1675 |
| 1615 | 1634 | 1657 | 1676 |
| 1616 | 1635 | 1658 | 1677 |
| 1617 | 1636 | | 1678 |
| 1618 | 1637 | 1659 | 1679 |
| 1619 | 1638 | 1660 | 1680 |
| 1620 | 1639 | 1661 | 1681 |
| 1621 | 1640 | 1662 | |
| 1622 | 1641 | | 1682 |
| 1623 | 1642 | 1663 | 1683 |
| 1624 | 1643 | 1664 | |
| | 1644 | 1665 | 1684 |
| 1625 | 1645 | | 1685 |
| 1626 | 1646 | 1666 | 1686 |
| | 1647 | 1667 | 1687 |
| | 1648 | 1668 | |

| Year | Mark | Year | Mark | Year | Mark | Year | Mark |
|---|---|---|---|---|---|---|---|
| 1688 | [letter] | 1778 | C | 1807 | V | 1835 | P |
| 1689 | [letter] | 1779 | D | | [mark] | 1836 | 3 |
| 1690 | [letter] | 1780 | E | 1808 | W | | [marks] |
| | [mark] | 1781 | F | 1809 | X | 1837 | A |
| 1691 | k | 1782 | G | 1810 | Y | 1838 | B |
| 1692 | l | 1783 | H | 1811 | Z | 1839 | C |
| 1693 | [letter] | 1784 | J [mark] | | [marks] | 1840 | D [mark] |
| | [mark] | 1785 | K | 1812 | a | 1841 | E |
| 1695 | [letter] | 1786 | L [mark] | 1813 | b | 1842 | F |
| 1696 | p | | [marks] | 1814 | c | 1843 | G |
| 1697 | [letter] | 1787 | A | 1815 | d | 1844 | H |
| 1698 | [letter] | 1788 | B | 1816 | e | 1845 | I |
| 1699 | S | 1789 | C C | 1817 | f | 1846 | K |
| | [marks] | 1790 | d | 1818 | g | 1847 | L |
| 1700 | A | 1791 | e | 1819 | h | 1848 | M |
| 1701 | B | 1792 | f | 1820 | i | 1849 | N |
| 1702 | C | 1793 | g | 1821 | k | 1850 | O |
| 1703 | D | 1794 | h | 1822 | l | | |
| 1704 | D | 1795 | i | 1823 | m | | |
| 1705 | F | 1796 | k [mark] | 1824 | n | | |
| 1706 | G | 1797 | L | 1825 | o | 1851 | P |
| 1707 | G | 1798 | M | 1826 | p | 1852 | Q |
| 1708 | [letter] | 1799 | N | 1927 | q | 1853 | R |
| 1709 | [letter] | 1800 | O | 1828 | r | 1854 | S |
| 1710 | [letter] | 1801 | P | 1829 | s | 1855 | T |
| 1711 | m | 1802 | Q | 1830 | t [mark] | 1856 | V |
| 1712 | [letter] | 1803 | R | 1831 | u | | |
| 1713 | [letter] | 1804 | S | 1832 | v | | |
| | [marks] | 1805 | T | 1833 | w | | |
| | | 1806 | U | 1834 | x | | |

Leopard's head not used after 1850

NEWCASTLE

## NEWCASTLE

Newcastle was granted power of assay by Henry VI's statute of 1423. The original mark was three separate castles in a shield. Marking was rather erratic until 1702 when the figure of Britannia and the lion's head erased, denoting the new standard, were introduced. In 1720, when the old standard was restored, the leopard's head and lion passant replaced the old mark, used with the town mark and date letter. From 1721 to 1727 the lion passant faces to the right. Substantial quantities of Newcastle silver date from the early 18th century, especially domestic ware, such as coffee pots and teapots. Large numbers of tankards and two-handled cups were also produced in this city. The last assay of silver at Newcastle was in April 1884.

| | | | | | |
|---|---|---|---|---|---|
| 1658 | | 1697 | 1715 | 1730 | |
| 1664 | | 1698 | 1716 | 1731 | |
| 1668 | | 1698-9 | 1717 | 1732 | |
| no mark found for 1669 | | 1700 | 1718 | 1733 | |
| 1670-2 | | 1701 | 1719 | 1734 | |
| 1672 | | 1702 | 1720 | 1735 | |
| 1675 | | 1703 | 1721 | 1736 | |
| 1680 | | 1704 | 1722 | 1737 | |
| 1684 | | 1705 | 1723 | 1738 | |
| 1684 | | 1706 | 1724 | 1739 | |
| 1684 | | 1707 | 1725 | 1740 | |
| 1685 | | 1708 | 1726 | 1741 | |
| 1685 | | 1709 | 1727 | 1742 | |
| 1686-7 | | 1710 | Between 1721–8 shapes of shields and lion passant vary; the lion may face left | 1743 | |
| 1686-8 | | 1711 | | 1744 | |
| 1692 | | 1712 | | 1745 | |
| 1694 | | 1713 | | 1746 | |
| 1694 | | | 1728 | 1747 | |
| 1694 | | 1714 | 1729 | 1748 | |
| 1695 | | | | 1749 | |

| Year | Mark | Year | Mark | Year | Mark | Year | Mark |
|---|---|---|---|---|---|---|---|
| 1750 | L | | 🛡️🦁👑 | 1806 | Q | 1835 | W |
| 1751 | M | 1779 | N | 1807 | R | 1836 | X |
| 1752 | N | 1780 | O | 1808 | S | 1837 | Y |
| 1753 | O | 1781 | P | 1809 | T | 1838 | Z |
| 1754 | P | 1782 | Q | 1810 | U | | 🦁🛡️👑👤 |
| 1755 | Q | 1783 | R | 1811 | W | 1839 | A |
| 1756 | R | 1784 | S👑 | 1812 | X | 1840 | B |
| 1757 | S | 1785 | T | 1813 | Y | 1841 | C👤 |
| 1758 | S | 1786 | U👤 | 1814 | Z | 1842 | D |
| | 🛡️🦁👑 | 1787 | W | | 🦁🛡️👑👤 | 1843 | E |
| 1759 | a | 1788 | X | 1815 | A | 1844 | F |
| 1760 | a | 1789 | Y | 1816 | B | 1845 | G |
| 1761 | a | 1790 | Z | 1817 | C | | 🦁🛡️👑👤 |
| 1762 | a | | 🦁🛡️👑👤 | 1818 | D | 1846 | H |
| 1763 | a | 1791 | A | 1819 | E | 1847 | I |
| 1764 | a | 1792 | B | 1820 | F | 1848 | J |
| 1765 | a | 1793 | C | 1821 | G👤 | 1849 | K |
| 1766 | a | 1794 | D | 1822 | H | 1850 | L |
| 1767 | a | 1795 | E | 1823 | I | 1851 | M |
| 1768 | a | 1796 | F | 1824 | K | 1852 | N |
| 1769 | a | 1797 | G | 1825 | L | 1853 | O |
| 1770 | a | 1798 | H | 1826 | M | 1854 | P |
| 1771 | a | 1799 | I | 1827 | N | 1855 | Q |
| 1772 | a | | 🦁🛡️👑👤 | 1828 | O | 1856 | R |
| 1773 | G | 1800 | K | 1829 | P | 1857 | S |
| 1774 | H | 1801 | L | 1830 | Q | 1858 | T |
| 1775 | I | 1802 | M | 1831 | R | 1859 | U |
| 1776 | K | 1803 | N👤 | 1832 | S👤 | 1860 | W |
| 1777 | L | 1804 | O | 1833 | T | 1861 | X |
| 1778 | M | 1805 | P | 1834 | U | 1862 | Y |

| 1863 | Ⓩ | 1868 | ⓔ | 1874 | ① | 1880 | ⓡ |
| | 🐟👑🔔○ | 1869 | ⓕ | 1875 | ⓜ | 1881 | ⓢ |
| 1864 | ⓐ | 1870 | ⓖ | 1876 | ⓝ | 1882 | ⓣ |
| 1865 | ⓑ | 1871 | ⓗ | 1877 | ⓞ | 1883 | ⓤ |
| 1866 | ⓒ | 1872 | ⓘ | 1878 | ⓟ | | |
| 1867 | ⓓ | 1873 | ⓚ | 1879 | ⓠ | | |

## GLASGOW

Glasgow had its own corporation of hammermen by 1536, and in 1681 they adopted a date letter system. However, this went out of use in the early 18th century, when the letters S (Sterling, or Scottish), O and E were frequently used, together with the town mark showing a tree with a bird in its upper branches, a bell suspended from a lower branch and a fish laid at the base. In 1819 the lion rampant of Scotland and the sovereign's head were added, and in 1914 the thistle standard mark was used. The Glasgow office closed in 1964, after running at a loss for some years. Silver marked with the early Glasgow hallmark is rarely seen.

| | | | | | | | |
|---|---|---|---|---|---|---|---|
| 1783 | | 1837 | Ⓢ | 1865 | | 1894 | Ⓧ |
| 1783 | | 1838 | Ⓣ | 1866 | | 1895 | Ⓨ |
| 1777-90 | | 1839 | Ⓤ | 1867 | | 1896 | Ⓩ |
| 1782-92 | | 1840 | Ⓥ | 1868 | | | |
| | | 1841 | Ⓦ | 1869 | | 1897 | Ⓐ |
| 1785-95 | | 1842 | Ⓧ | 1870 | | 1898 | Ⓑ |
| 1785-95 | | 1843 | Ⓨ | | | 1899 | Ⓒ |
| 1781 | | 1844 | Ⓩ | 1871 | Ⓐ | 1900 | Ⓓ |
| 1811-3 | | | | 1872 | Ⓑ | 1901 | Ⓔ |
| | | 1845 | Ⓐ | 1873 | Ⓒ | 1902 | Ⓕ |
| 1819 | Ⓐ | 1846 | Ⓑ | 1874 | Ⓓ | 1903 | Ⓖ |
| | | 1847 | Ⓒ | 1875 | Ⓔ | 1904 | Ⓗ |
| 1820 | Ⓑ | 1848 | Ⓓ | 1876 | Ⓕ | 1905 | Ⓘ |
| 1821 | Ⓒ | 1849 | Ⓔ | 1877 | Ⓖ | 1906 | Ⓙ |
| 1822 | Ⓓ | 1850 | Ⓕ | 1878 | Ⓗ | 1907 | Ⓚ |
| 1823 | Ⓔ | 1851 | Ⓖ | 1879 | Ⓘ | 1908 | Ⓛ |
| 1824 | Ⓕ | 1852 | Ⓗ | 1880 | Ⓙ | 1909 | Ⓜ |
| 1825 | Ⓖ | | | 1881 | Ⓚ | 1910 | Ⓝ |
| 1826 | Ⓗ | 1853 | Ⓘ | 1882 | Ⓛ | 1911 | Ⓞ |
| 1827 | Ⓘ | 1854 | Ⓙ | 1883 | Ⓜ | 1912 | Ⓟ |
| 1828 | Ⓙ | 1855 | Ⓚ | 1884 | Ⓝ | 1913 | Ⓠ |
| 1829 | Ⓚ | 1856 | Ⓛ | 1885 | Ⓞ | | |
| 1830 | Ⓛ | 1857 | Ⓜ | 1886 | Ⓟ | 1914 | Ⓡ |
| 1831 | Ⓜ | 1858 | Ⓝ | 1887 | Ⓠ | 1915 | Ⓢ |
| 1832 | Ⓝ | 1859 | Ⓞ | 1888 | Ⓡ | 1916 | Ⓣ |
| 1833 | Ⓞ | 1860 | Ⓟ | 1889 | Ⓢ | 1917 | Ⓤ |
| 1834 | Ⓟ | 1861 | Ⓠ | 1890 | Ⓣ | 1918 | Ⓥ |
| 1835 | Ⓠ | 1862 | Ⓡ | 1891 | Ⓤ | 1919 | Ⓦ |
| 1836 | Ⓡ | 1863 | Ⓢ | 1892 | Ⓥ | 1920 | Ⓧ |
| | | 1864 | Ⓣ | 1893 | Ⓦ | 1921 | Ⓨ |

**GLASGOW/CHESTER**

| | | | | | |
|---|---|---|---|---|---|
| 1922 | Z | 1929 | g | 1935 | m |
| 1923 | a | 1930 | h | 1936 | n |
| 1924 | b | 1931 | i | 1937 | o |
| 1925 | c | 1932 | j | 1938 | p |
| 1926 | d | 1933 | k | 1939 | q |
| 1927 | e | 1934 | l | | |
| 1928 | f | | | | |

## CHESTER

There are records in town deeds of silversmiths working in Chester as early as the 13th century. Marking of silver was not regulated until the end of the 17th century, even though there was a guild of goldsmiths who supervised the manufacture, assay and sale of plate from the early 15th century.

Chester's town mark showed a shield bearing the arms of the city. The accompanying marks were similar to those of London of the same period, with the lion passant, leopard's head and date letter. The majority of silverware found now bearing the Chester mark consists of smallware such as tankards, beakers, tumblers and cream jugs. The office stopped operating on 24 August 1962.

| | | | | | | | |
|---|---|---|---|---|---|---|---|
| 1683 | STERLING | 1695 | D | 1709 | I | 1720 | U |
| 1685 | Sterlg | 1696 | E | 1710 | K | 1721 | V |
| 1686 | | 1697 | F | 1711 | L | 1722 | W |
| 1687 | | 1701 | A | 1712 | M | 1723 | X |
| 1688 | | 1702 | B | 1713 | N | 1724 | Y |
| 1689 | | 1703 | C | 1714 | O | 1725 | Z |
| 1690-2 | | 1704 | D | 1715 | P | | |
| 1690-2 | | 1705 | E | 1716 | Q | 1726 | A |
| 1690-2 | | 1706 | F | 1717 | R | 1727 | B |
| 1692 | STERLING | 1707 | G | 1718 | S | 1728 | C |
| 1692-4 | STERLING | 1708 | H | 1719 | T | 1729 | D |
| 1695-1700 | STERLING | | | | | 1730 | G |

| | | | | | | | |
|---|---|---|---|---|---|---|---|
| 1731 | 𝕵 | 1760 | 𝕜 | 1787 | 𝕞 | 1815 | 𝕋 |
| 1732 | 𝕲 | 1761 | 𝕝 | 1788 | 𝕟 | 1816 | 𝕌 |
| 1733 | 𝕳 | 1762 | 𝕞 | 1789 | 𝕠 | 1817 | 𝕍 |
| 1734 | 𝕴 | 1763 | 𝕟 | 1790 | 𝕡 | | 🛡🛡🛡🛡 |
| 1735 | 𝕶 | 1764 | 𝕠 | 1791 | 𝕢 | 1818 | Ⓐ |
| 1736 | 𝕷 | 1765 | 𝕻 | 1792 | 𝕣 | 1819 | Ⓑ |
| 1737 | 𝕸 | 1766 | 𝕼 | 1793 | 𝕤 | 1820 | Ⓒ |
| 1738 | 𝕹 | 1767 | 𝕽 | 1794 | 𝕥 | 1821 | Ⓓ |
| 1739 | 𝕺 | 1768 | 𝕾 | 1795 | 𝕦 | 1822 | Ⓓ |
| 1740 | 𝕻 | 1769 | 𝕿 | 1796 | 𝕍 | | 🛡🛡🛡🛡 |
| 1741 | 𝕼 | 1770 | 𝖀 | | 🛡🛡🛡🛡 | 1823 | Ⓔ |
| 1742 | 𝕽 | 1771 | 𝖀 | 1797 | Ⓐ | 1824 | Ⓕ |
| 1743 | 𝕾 | 1772 | 𝖁 | 1798 | Ⓑ | 1825 | Ⓖ |
| 1744 | 𝕿 | 1773 | 𝖂 | 1799 | Ⓒ | 1826 | Ⓗ |
| 1745 | 𝖀 | 1774 | 𝖃 | | 🛡🛡🛡🛡 | 1827 | Ⓘ |
| 1746 | 𝖁 | 1775 | 𝖄 | 1800 | Ⓓ | 1828 | Ⓚ |
| 1747 | 𝖂 | | 🛡🛡🛡 | 1801 | Ⓔ | 1829 | Ⓛ |
| 1748 | 𝖃 | 1776 | ⓐ | 1802 | Ⓕ | 1830 | Ⓜ |
| 1749 | 𝖄𝖁 | 1777 | ⓑ | 1803 | Ⓖ | 1831 | Ⓝ |
| 1750 | 𝖅 | 1778 | ⓒ | 1804 | Ⓗ | 1832 | Ⓞ |
| 🛡🛡🛡 | | | 🛡🛡🛡🛡 | 1805 | Ⓘ | 1833 | Ⓟ |
| 1751 | ⓐ | 1779 | ⓓ | 1806 | Ⓚ | 1834 | Ⓠ |
| 1752 | ⓑ | 1780 | ⓔ | 1807 | Ⓛ | 1835 | Ⓡ |
| 1753 | ⓒ | 1781 | ⓕ | 1808 | Ⓜ | 1836 | Ⓢ |
| 1754 | ⓓ | 1782 | ⓖ | 1809 | Ⓝ | 1837 | Ⓣ |
| 1755 | ⓔ | 1783 | ⓗ | 1810 | Ⓞ | 1838 | Ⓤ |
| 1756 | ⓕ | | 🛡🛡🛡🛡 | 1811 | Ⓟ | | 🛡🛡🛡 |
| 1757 | ⓖ | 1784 | ⓘ | 1812 | Ⓠ | 1839 | Ⓐ |
| 1758 | ⓗ | 1785 | ⓚ | 1813 | Ⓡ | 1840 | Ⓑ |
| 1759 | ⓘ | 1786 | ⓘ | 1814 | Ⓢ | 1841 | Ⓒ |

**CHESTER**

| Year | Mark | Year | Mark | Year | Mark | Year | Mark |
|------|------|------|------|------|------|------|------|
| 1842 | 🛡 | 1871 | h | 1899 | Q | 1927 | b |
| 1843 | | 1872 | i | 1900 | R | 1928 | c |
| 1844 | F | 1873 | k | [town marks] | | 1929 | d |
| 1845 | | 1874 | l | 1901 | A | 1930 | e |
| 1846 | | 1875 | m | 1902 | B | 1931 | ff |
| 1847 | | 1876 | n | 1903 | C | 1932 | g |
| 1848 | R | 1877 | o | 1904 | D | [town marks] | |
| 1849 | L | 1878 | p | 1905 | E | 1933 | h |
| 1850 | | 1879 | q | 1906 | F | 1934 | i |
| 1851 | | 1880 | r | 1907 | G | 1935 | k |
| 1852 | | 1881 | s | 1908 | H | [town marks] | |
| 1853 | | 1882 | t | 1909 | I | 1936 | l |
| 1854 | | 1883 | u | 1910 | K | 1937 | m |
| 1855 | R | [town marks] | | 1911 | L | 1938 | n |
| 1856 | S | 1884 | A | 1912 | M | 1939 | o |
| 1857 | | 1885 | B | 1913 | N | | |
| 1858 | | 1886 | C | 1914 | O | | |
| 1859 | | 1887 | D | 1915 | P | | |
| 1860 | | 1888 | E | 1916 | Q | | |
| 1861 | | 1889 | F | 1917 | R | | |
| 1862 | | [town marks] | | 1918 | S | | |
| 1863 | | 1890 | G | 1919 | T | | |
| [town marks] | | 1891 | H | 1920 | U | | |
| 1864 | | 1892 | I | 1921 | V | | |
| 1865 | b | 1893 | K | 1922 | W | | |
| 1866 | c | 1894 | L | 1923 | X | | |
| 1867 | d | 1895 | M | 1924 | Y | | |
| 1868 | e | 1896 | N | 1925 | Z | | |
| 1869 | f | 1897 | O | [town marks] | | | |
| 1870 | g | 1898 | P | 1926 | a | | |

# ASSAY OFFICES – MINOR

**Barnstaple** Goldsmiths worked in Barnstaple as early as 1370 and are recorded until the end of the 17th century. The earliest mark used from 1272 until c1624 was adapted from the borough mark, which showed a bird in a circular stamp. It later changed to a triple-turreted tower derived from the city's arms and was used until the end of the 17th century.

**Bristol** The city was appointed an Assay Office by the Act of 1701 but there are no traces of an assay office or of a guild of goldsmiths. Some marks have been found with the Bristol arms (a ship issuing from a castle) included, but their origin is not yet confirmed.

**Carlisle** Marks dating from the 16th and 17th century, showing a single four-petalled rose, have been identified as the marks of the city of Carlisle. A similar rose appears in the arms of the city.

**Coventry** The town mark was thought to be an animal in outline, possibly an elephant, but this was later attributed to the Devon and Cornwall goldsmiths. There are four pewter plates which bear the Coventry arms.

**Hull** Early pieces made in Hull are marked with the letter H as the town mark; this was replaced in the 17th century by the town arms showing three ducal coronets. It is unlikely that there was an assay office here, but its distance from London and other towns made the registering of its own marks practical.

**King's Lynn** The town arms of King's Lynn were adapted to make the town mark. This shows three dragons' heads with crosses in their mouths on a shield background. Marks have been recorded from here from c1632.

**Leeds** Leeds goldsmiths adopted the arms of the town, showing a golden fleece, for its town mark. The mark is usually found on wares dating from the 17th century.

**Leicester** Silversmiths were active from the early 16th until the 17th century. The town mark showed a cinquefoil, taken from the city's coat-of-arms.

**Lewes**  Lewes silversmiths marked their wares with a chequered shield derived from the town seal, which showed a lion rampant in the right-hand corner. Spoons bearing this mark survive from the late 16th and early 17th century.

**Lincoln**  The city was granted power of assay by Henry VI's statute of 1423, although silversmiths are known to have worked in Lincoln from the 12th century onwards. The town mark was derived from the city arms and depicted a fleur-de-lys. The mark is most commonly found on spoons.

**Plymouth**  Plymouth marks date from c1600 to c1700, when the city's arms were adapted to make a town mark showing a saltire between four castles. This mark is usually found on spoons. From the early 18th century the goldsmiths used the assay office of Exeter to register marks.

**Poole**  Marks depicting a scallop shell, dating from the 16th and 17th centuries, have been identified as the coat-of-arms of Poole. Three similar shells appear in the town arms.

**Salisbury**  The city was granted power of assay by Henry VI's statute of 1423. However, there are no marks found that can be definitely associated with this city and there is no evidence of a guild of goldsmiths. Some spoons were found in various parts of Wiltshire that bear marks that have been ascribed to Salisbury.

**Sherborne**  Although there is no known town mark, there are records of one famous local goldsmith, Richard Orenge, who used marks from 1572 to 1607 depicting his initials and a central pellet, surrounded by two concentric circles of pellets.

**Taunton**  Evidence of goldsmiths using the town mark of a 'T' and a tun can be found on apostle spoons and a paten, dating between 1665 and 1689.

**Truro**  A mark showing the initials TR surrounded by a circle of pellets found on Cornish spoons of the 17th century is thought to be the town mark of Truro.

# EUROPEAN HALLMARKING

The English hallmarking system did not extend to the Continent of Europe where, because of almost constant wars between nations, silver was frequently melted down to pay for armies and war debts. Europe used various standards – the only examples seen today are 800, 830 and 900 parts per thousand. These are usually shown by a small stamp somewhere on a piece. Such stamps do not necessarily correspond to contemporary English silver standards, and consequently objects with Continental marks are often sold under the name 'Continental silver', or 'silver-coloured metal'.

In France, a form of guaranteeing marks was first used as early as 1272; however, despite the introduction of the silver standard by Charles V in 1378, the system developed haphazardly and marking remained somewhat arbitrary. French silverwares may exhibit a community mark (struck by the *gardes de la communauté* or community wardens, the equivalent of the English master of the touch, and confirming the standard of fineness), a maker's mark (usually consisting of his initials and emblem), a city mark (again, the responsibility of the community wardens) and a juranda mark (the French equivalent of the date letter system). A few other marks also appear. The charge mark, which appeared in 1672, was struck by the *fermier du droit*, or tax farmer, to confirm that any tax payable on the article had been noted and would be collected; the discharge mark confirms the payment of any such tax.

Minor marks used on French silver include the inventory or census mark. If a newly-appointed tax farmer adopted a different mark from that of his predecessor, the wares stamped by the retiring tax farmer were catalogued in a general inventory and countermarked with an inventory mark.

Silver imported to France was stamped ET, for *étranger* (foreign), while the recognition mark, introduced in 1750, was stamped on any new parts added to old pieces of silverware.

In Germany and Austria, a system was developed to denote the town of production, the maker and year letters, but these follow no reliable order. Similarly, although a silver standard existed in theory, it was not always strictly observed.

In medieval Russia, every large monastic foundation had its own silversmith, and from the 17th century onwards all silver belonging to the patriarchs was stamped with the blessing hand. From 1613, all silver sold at fairs had to be marked, and in 1700 Peter the Great introduced a gold and silver standard to be overseen by assay offices established in all Russian towns.

**BELGIUM**

Swedish silver was stamped with a mark representing the town of assay and a date letter. The Swiss system was more developed and the degrees of refinement of silver were indicated by a stamp. Some European countries have developed a silver hallmarking system only very recently. Romania passed a law as recently as 1906 that silver must bear the maker's mark and a hallmark.

## BELGIUM

From the mid-16th century, silversmiths in Brussels, Artois (Northern France, now Belgium), Luxembourg and the Netherlands were regulated by order of Emperor Charles V. By the 17th century silver was marked with a town mark, date letter and maker's mark. Hallmarking became obligatory in 1831. After 1869 assaying was no longer customary and any standard of purity was permitted. State marks indicating purity were introduced.

**Antwerp** Variations on this mark used from the early 16th to late 18th century. A date letter system was used between the 17th and 18th centuries.

Early 18thC

| | | | | |
|---|---|---|---|---|
| 1609 | 16th/17thC | 17thC | 17thC | 1619 |
| 17thC | 17thC | 17thC | 17thC | 1662–63 |
| 1662–63 | 17thC | 1664 | 1669 | 17thC |
| 1680 | 17thC | 1738 | 1765 | 1772 |

**Bruges** Similar marks used early 16th to 18th centuries.

1660

1777

17thC

18thC

**Brussels** Similar marks used between the 17th and 18th centuries.

1658          1764          Early 18thC

**Ghent** Similar marks used between the 16th and late 18th centuries.

Early 18thC          1752          1787

**Liège** Various marks within a shield used between the 16th and 18th centuries. Sometimes date appears in mark.

1688/94          1693          1744          1764          1784

**Louvain** A key or a shield surmounted by a crown used between the 15th and 18th centuries. Letter B or V also sometimes found.

1710          18thC          1777

**Mons** Similar mark or letters AE surmounted by a crown used between the 15th and 18th centuries. Last two letters of date surmounted by crown also sometimes found.

1730          1750          1766          1776/79          1779          1793

**Tournai** Castle turret, letter T surmounted by a crown, or three fleurs-de-lys surmounted by a crown used between the 16th and 18th centuries. Last two letters of date surmounted by crown also used.

Early 18thC

Early 18thC

Early 18thC

1737

1740

1781

**Ypres** Similar marks used between the early 16th century and mid-18th century. Letter Y surmounted by crown used in the late 18th century.

1701–13

1712

1745–50

Late 18thC

**Hallmarks used 1814–31**

Large Objects

Small Objects

Large Objects

Small Objects

**Hallmarks used 1831–68**

Purity

.950

.800

Hallmark

Large Objects

Small Objects

## Hallmarks used 1869–1942

Large Objects  Small Objects

.900     .800        .900     .800

## Hallmarks used from 1942 onwards

Large Objects  Small Objects

.900     .800        .900     .800

## DENMARK

Danish silver was marked with a city or town mark from the 17th century. From the late 17th century silver had four marks: town mark, assayer's mark (usually his initials in a square or oval cartouche), mark of the month (sign of the zodiac) and maker's mark. Copenhagen's mark usually incorporates the date. From 1888, Danish silver of a purity of .826 was stamped with an official mark showing the three towers of Copenhagen in an oval and the last two numbers of the year the piece was assayed.

**Copenhagen** The three towers of Copenhagen in an oval shield with date below were used between the early 17th and the 19th centuries. Usually only the last two numbers of the date appear after 1771. Only the last number appears between 1801 and 1809.

1762     1799     1808     1850     1859

**Aalborg** Three towers in an oval shield, sometimes with date, used between the mid-17th and the 19th centuries. Mark becomes more stylized in the 19th century.

00

**Aarhus**  Similar mark used during 18th and 19th centuries. Name in full in rectangle also used.

18thC            19thC

**Odense**  Similar mark with or without date in shield of varying shape found between the 17th and 19th centuries. Name in full also used.

**Viborg**  Two marks used from 17th to 18th century. Name in full used in 19th century.

18thC                          19thC

**Month marks**

Zodiacal symbols used to indicate month of manufacture.

**Hallmark since 1888**

.826 purity

## FRANCE

Most French silver has four marks: maker's mark, community or warden's mark, charge mark and discharge mark.

From the early 16th century, silver objects made in Paris were stamped with crowned letters by the wardens of the silversmiths' guild – La Maison Commune – who were responsible for maintaining the purity of silver. The letters changed annually with each warden; some letters such as 'J' and 'U' were omitted.

| | | | |
|---|---|---|---|
| 1697–1717 | C – Z (no J or U) | 1764–84 | A – U (no J) |
| 1717–39 | A – Z (no J or U) | 1784–89 | P (in various sizes) |
| 1740–63 | A – Z (no J or U) | | |

**Examples of community marks of the Paris Maison Commune**

1729

1734

1752

1758

1764

1786

1789

1789

**A similar crowned P mark in various styles used from 1784**

## Charge and discharge marks

When silver was assayed (usually in parts) it was marked
with a charge mark. This showed that the piece was of the
required standard and that duty was owed on the item.
City charge marks were usually a letter – the letter for Paris
was A – and their changing style can help with dating,
although the marks are easily confused with some
community marks used (see above). In the smaller
provincial centres, a charge mark was often the town's
arms or initials.

When the tax owed was paid to the tax farmer the piece
was stamped with a discharge mark. Discharge marks also
varied according to the region and often differ according
to the size of the article.

This system of marking was abolished in 1791, in the
aftermath of the 1789 French Revolution. Control over
the standard of silver was re-established in 1797. Tax was
collected by the State from this date on, and silver was
marked with a more uniform system.

## City Letter Charge Marks

| | | | | | | | |
|---|---|---|---|---|---|---|---|
| A | Paris | H | La Rochelle | P | Dijon | X | Amiens |
| B | Rouen | I | Limoges | Q | Perpignan | Y | Bourges |
| | Caen | K | Bordeaux | R | Orleans | Z | Grenoble |
| | Lyon | L | Bayonne | S | Reims | & | Aix |
| | Tours | M | Toulouse | T | Nantes | AA | Metz |
| | ngers | N | Montpellier | V | Troyes | CC | Besançon |
| | itiers | O | Riom | W | Lille | 9 | Rennes |

**...ividual city entries on following pages
...niles of city charge marks.)**

## Paris
### Charge marks

1684–87

charge

discharge

1687–91

charge

discharge

1691–98

charge

discharge

1697–1703

charge

discharge

1704–12

charge

discharge

1713–17

charge

discharge

charge

discharge

1717–22

charge

discharge

1722–27

charge

discharge

1727–32

charge

discharge

1732–38

charge               discharge

1738–44

charge               discharge

1744–50

charge               discharge

1750–56

charge               discharge

1756–62

charge               discharge

1762–68

charge               discharge

1769–75

charge               discharge

**FRANCE**

1775–81

charge                       discharge

1781–89

charge                                   discharge

1789

charge     discharge

## REGIONAL MARKS

**Aix**                  1750

charge

1774–80

charge   discharge            charge   discharge

1780–90

charge   discharge

1780–91                    1780 community

charge   discharge

## Amiens

1737–39

community

1764–74

charge

1762–68

discharge

1768–74

community

1784–91

community

**Angers** Letter H surmounted by crown 1716–71.
ANGERS appears in 1748, 1750, 1754. It appears with
letter 1774–83.

1768–74

charge

1734–41

discharge

1716

community

1774

1784–89

**Bordeaux** Letter K in various styles surmounted by crown
used from 17th century until 1789. Various discharge
marks used. Letters BOR with date letter appear in most
community marks 17th to early 18th century when it is
replaced by the letter B and date letter.

1691–98 charge

1691–98 community

1689–1703 charge

1698–1703 community

1780–89

charge

discharge

1780–89

·harge

discharge

1780 community

**Dijon** Letter P in various styles used between the late 17th and late 18th centuries. Discharge marks vary.

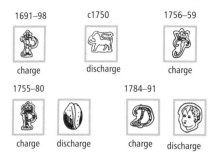

1691–98
charge

c1750
discharge

1756–59
charge

1755–80
charge    discharge

1784–91
charge    discharge

**Grenoble** Similar marks used between 1600–1760. Last two numbers of date used from c1784.

Community marks
1716–18    1741    1784

**Lille** Similar mark or date letter surmounted by a crown used in 18th century.

1750    1775    1770

**Lyons** Letter D in various styles from 17th century and the 1780s. Community mark shows lion rampant surmounted by crown with date letter 1712–77. Later marks vary.

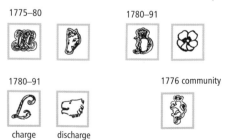

1775–80    1780–91

1780–91
charge    discharge

1776 community

**Metz** Shield with date letter used in mid-18th century. AA or M used during late 18th century.

1774–80     mid-18thC     1780–91

charge    discharge     community     charge    discharge

**Montpellier** Letters MP intertwined or letter N used for charge mark during 18th century. Date letter surmounted by a crown above letters MPL used as community mark from 1709–82.

1709        1774–80

community     charge    discharge

1780–91

charge    discharge     18thC

**Nancy** Similar mark used throughout 18th century.

c.1790        late 18thC

**Nantes** Letter T used as charge mark until mid-18th century when word NANTES appears within a shield.

1744     1746      1762–69     1772

charge    discharge     charge    community

**Orléans** Letter R used as a charge mark from 1732 until c1780. Various community marks used.

early 18thC       1751–62

community       charge    discharge

**Poitiers**  Three Ps and a date letter used as a community mark during 18th century. Letter G surmounted by a crown in various styles used as charge mark between the 17th and late 18th centuries.

1744  1774–80

community    charge    discharge

**Reims**  Letter S used as charge mark between c1768 and the late-18th century. Various community marks used.

c1750  1768–74

community    charge    discharge

1768–74  1784–91

**Rennes**  Number 9 in various styles used as charge mark between the late 17th century and late 18th century.

1721 discharge    1725 community    1754–6 community

1756–62 charge    1780–89 charge    discharge

**Riom**  Letter O used as charge mark during 18th century. Community marks vary.

1775–80 community    1780–89 charge    discharge

**La Rochelle**  Letters H or LR intertwined used as a charge mark. Various community marks used.

1774–80

charge    discharge    charge    discharge

18thC community

**Rouen** Letter B surmounted by crown used as charge mark from late 17th century. Letter surmounted by crown used as community mark.

1774–80 charge    discharge

18thC community

**Strasbourg** Similar marks showing shield surmounted with fleur-de-lys and number 13 used between the mid-17th century and 1796. Sometimes a crown surmounts the number.

1725        1750–96        1752 date mark  1796

**Toulouse** Letter M used as charge mark from 16th century. Letters TOL surmounting a date letter in a shield used as a community mark between the late 17th and the late 18th centuries.

1768–74   1776                    1780–89

charge    community          charge    discharge

**Tours** Letter E surmounted by crown used as charge mark from early 18th century. Community marks show various crowned letters.

1739        1768–74        1774–80

community    charge          charge    discharge

**FRANCE**

1780–89 discharge marks

### Later French Marks

1793–94   1795–97

1797   1798

1798–1809

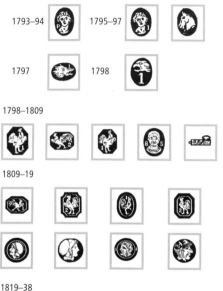

1809–19

1819–38

1879 onwards

## GERMANY

Silver was marked in Germany from the 15th century. German silver submitted for assay was marked to indicate its maker and town of origin. Town marks changed slightly over the centuries and can help with dating. Nuremberg, Königsberg and Dresden also had date letter systems. There was no consistent purity guarantee for German silver before 1884. Since then, purity has been indicated in numbers, expressed as thousandths, and the crown and crescent mark of Germany denotes a purity of at least .80

**Augsburg** Variations on mark used between 16th century and 1800.

1767–69

**Berlin** Variations on bear mark used between the late 17th and 19th centuries. Date letter appears after c1750.

early 18thC     19thC

**Cologne** Similar marks used 17th to late 18th centuries.

late 17thC      late 18thC

**Dantzig** Variations on mark used between the 16th and 18th centuries.

17th/18thC

**Dresden** Variations used from 18th century to mid-19th century. DRESDEN sometimes appears in full on later pieces.

early 18thC    late 18thC    19thC

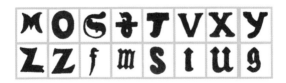

Date letters found on Dresden silver of the 18th to 19th centuries.

**Düsseldorf** Anchor mark only used during 17th and 18th century. Anchor with lion, sometimes surmounted by a number 12 or 13, used during 18th century.

18thC

**Essen** Similar mark used from 17th century to 18th century.

17th/18thC

**GERMANY**

**Frankfurt** Similar mark used between the 16th and the late 18th centuries.

17th/18thC

mid-18thC

**Hamburg** Similar mark on shield of varying background used between the 16th and 19th centuries.

17th/18thC

**Hanover** Similar mark with last two numbers of date used from 2nd half of 17th century to mid-18th century.

mid-18thC

**Königsberg** Similar mark used between the late 17th and mid-19th centuries.

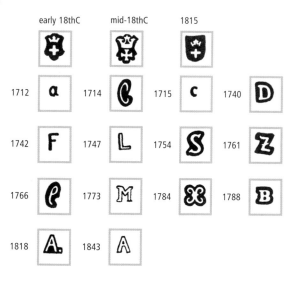

early 18thC     mid-18thC     1815

1712 a    1714    1715 c    1740 D

1742 F    1747 L    1754 S    1761 Z

1766    1773 M    1784    1788 B

1818 A.    1843 A

**Leipzig** Letter L used between the 16th and 17th centuries. Crossed swords with letter L and number 12 used between the 17th and 18th centuries.

17thC

17th/18thC

**Lubeck** Similar mark used between the 16th and 18th centuries.

18thC

**Luneburg** Similar mark with shield of varying shape used between the early 16th and the 17th centuries. Crescent moon with number 12 in circle used in early 19th century.

mid-17thC      early 19thC

**Magdeburg** Castle of varying design used between the early 17th and the 18th centuries.

early 18thC

**Mannheim** Similar marks recorded during 18th century.

early 18thC      late 18thC

**Munich** Similar mark used from late 17th century. Date appears with figure between 1742 and 1795.

18thC      mid-18thC

### Nuremberg

date letters

| late 18thC | early 19thC | 1766–69 | 1769–73 |
|---|---|---|---|
|  |  |  |  |

| 1773–76 | 1776–80 | 1780–83 | 1783–87 |
|---|---|---|---|
|  |  |  |  |

| 1787–90 | 1790–94 | 1794–97 | 1797–1800 |
|---|---|---|---|
|  |  |  |  |

| 19thC | | | |
|---|---|---|---|
|  |  |  |  |

**Prussia**

1809

**Regensburg**

18thC

mid-17thC

**Strasbourg**  Similar mark used between the 16th and mid-17th centuries.

**Stuttgart**  Similar mark used between late 16th to 19th century. Date letter appears from late 18th century.

| late 17thC | early 18thC | late 18thC | 19thC |
|---|---|---|---|
|  |  |  |  |

**Uberlingen**  Similar mark used 16th to 18th centuries.

18thC

**Ulm**  Similar mark on shield of varying shape used between the 16th and 18th centuries.

| 17thC | early 18thC | 18thC |
|---|---|---|
|  |  |  |

**Purity mark for German silver made after 1888**

### ITALY

A uniform system of marking began in 1810 when assay offices were established in Milan, Venice, Ancona, Verona and Brescia. Before this, many towns adopted their own hallmarks. From 1873 hallmarking was adopted throughout the country. Purity was not obligatory but marks denoting purities of .950, .900 and .800 were used. New standards of .925 and .800 were introduced in 1935.

## Florence

17th–18thC                                18thC

**Genoa** Similar mark used between the 16th and 18th centuries.

18thC

## Milan

1810

**Naples** Marks showing letters NAP sometimes surmounted by a crown used between the 15th and mid-18th centuries. Last three numbers of date sometimes appear.

1716                           1720

## Palermo

18thC     

**Rome** Crossed keys mark used between the 17th century and late 18th century.

late 17thC                           late 18thC

**Hallmarks of purity used from early 18th century**

**ITALY**

**Turin** Similar mark used in
18th and 19th century.

1809

**Venice** Marks very varied, some
19th century marks include date.

17th–18thC

1805

1810–15

### Assay marks in Genoa, Appenines and Montenotte

.950

.900

.800

### Modern silver marks (after 1934)

## NETHERLANDS

From the mid-17th century silver was marked with maker's
mark, date letter, town mark, assayer's mark and a hallmark
showing the crowned lion which guaranteed the purity of
.875. New purity standards of .934 and .833 were used
between 1806–10. The Netherlands adopted French
marking systems from 1811 until 1953.

### Amsterdam

mid-17thC

early 18thC

**Arnhem** Similar mark used from 17th to 18th century.
Letters HOLS also sometimes appears.

18thC

**den Bosch** late 18thC

**Dortrecht** Various marks used in 18th century.

18thC

**Gouda**     17thC

**Maestricht**     18thC

**Rotterdam** City arms or lion rampant surmounted by crown used between the 17th and 18th centuries.

18thC

**Utrecht**     17thC

**Zwolle** Crossed shield appears in mark between the early 17th and early 19th centuries.

late 18thC–early 19thC

**Assay Office Marks**

Amsterdam

Arnhem

den Bosch

Delft

Dortrecht

Gouda

The Hague

Rotterdam

Utrecht

Zwolle

**Purity marks from 1810–14**

large .950     .800        small .800

**Purity marks from 1810–1953**

large .934     .833        small .833

**Tax marks**

**Date letters from 1814–1962**

1814     1834     1835     1859     1860

1884     1885     1909     1910     1934

1935     1944–Nov 1945     Nov 1945– 1947     1948–July     July–1949

**Marks on silver made after 1953**

large .925     .835     small .835     .800

## NORWAY

Early Norwegian marks usually comprised a city mark, the date (or a letter designating the year). From the mid-17th century to the mid-18th century, silver production was controlled by the king and the guilds were abolished. From 1766 silver was marked with a monthly mark, expressed either as a fraction or as a sign of the zodiac. A city mark, with seven balls and the date, was used from 1781 in Bergen. Many date marks show only the last two numbers of the date.

**Bergen** Letter B surmounted by crown in shield of varying shape used from 1580 to 1686. From 1740 to 1802, city gate, sometimes with date, used. Mark became increasingly stylized during 19th century. Mid-century mark shows only seven balls.

1767     1802     1856

**Oslo**     1647

**Trondheim** Similar flower mark used between the early 18th and the mid-19th centuries.

1744     1746     1860

**Date Marks**
During the 19th century date marks sometimes appear in full or are shown by last two numbers of the year.

1802     1832     1843

**Monthly Marks**
From 1740–65 monthly marks were shown as signs of the zodiac. From 1766 to 1820, fractions of 12 showed the month.

Dec 21–Jan 21     Jan 21–Feb 18     Feb 18–Mar 20

| Mar 20–Apr 20 | Apr 20–May 21 | May 22–June 21 |
|---|---|---|

| June 21–July 22 | July 22–Aug 21 | Aug 21–Sept 23 |
|---|---|---|

| Sept 23–Oct 23 | Oct 23–Nov 22 | Nov 22–Dec 21 |
|---|---|---|

**Purity marks**

**Norway (since 1893)
purity .830–.925**

.830–.925

## PORTUGAL

Before 1881 Portuguese silver was marked with a maker's mark and a town mark which guaranteed a purity of .958. Town marks usually consisted of the first letter of the town concerned within a shield of varying form. State hallmarking was introduced in 1881 and purity standards of .916 and .833 were obligatory from 1886. New hallmarking systems were introduced in 1938 and continue to this day.

**Braga**  Similar mark used between the late 17th and late 18th centuries.   late 18thC

**Coimbra**  Similar mark used between the late 17th and late 18th centuries.   late 18thC

**Evora**  Letter E in various styles used between first half of the 18th century and the early 19th century.   1738

**Faro**   19thC

**Guimaraes**  Letter G in mid-18thC shield of varying shape used between the mid-18th and mid-19th centuries.   Mid-18thC

**Lisbon**  Letter L used in shield of varying shape between the late 17th and late 19th centuries.

late 17thC          early 18thC          early 19thC

**Oporto**  Letter P used in shield of varying shape between the late 17th and late 19th centuries.

late 17thC      early 18thC      1791–1810      1836–43

**Purity marks used 1886–88**

Lisbon           Oporto

**Purity marks used 1886–1938**

Lisbon            Oporto

large .916      .833          large .916      .833

Lisbon            Oporto

small .916      .833          small .916      .833

**Marks used from 1938**

Lisbon           Oporto

### RUSSIA

In Moscow, silver had been marked from 1613. The first mark showed a two-headed eagle. In 1684 the eagle was replaced with a purity mark and date mark inside a circle. The eagle returned to use from 1700–10 and carried a sceptre and orb. Assay offices were established in Moscow and St Petersburg during the first half of the 18th century. Throughout the 18th and 19th centuries silver made in Moscow or St Petersburg was marked by the maker, the guild, and the assay office where it was stamped with the mark of the assayer and the office. From 1729 in Moscow, the date was stamped separately and the assayer's initials were marked beneath the eagle. From 1733 the word MOCKBA apppeared under the eagle. After 1741 a new mark showing St George killing the dragon was introduced.

Provincial silver was marked with the town mark, maker's mark and a mark of purity in figures in a rectangular shield. A comprehensive system of marking was introduced in 1891; this included the initials of the assayer and a woman's head.

## Moscow

| 1696 | 1702 | 1728 |
| --- | --- | --- |

| 1731 | 1741 |
| --- | --- |

| 1782 | 1880 |
| --- | --- |

### Assayers' marks

| 1841 | 1875–80 | 1890–95 |
| --- | --- | --- |

**Astrakhan**  Similar mark used in shield of varying shape between the 18th and 19th centuries.

1828

**Kiev**  Name in full appears during 18th century. New mark, sometimes incorporating date, introduced in early 19th century.

| 1735–74 | 1828–87 | 1848–65 | 1825–47 |
| --- | --- | --- | --- |

# Novgorod

1717–32

1851–62

**Similar mark used from 1738–1862**

1864

**Odessa**  Anchor mark used during 19th century.

1843–4

19thC

**Petrograd (St Petersburg)**  City arms mark used with date until 1825, after which date no longer appeared.

1700–30

1730–40

1742

**Vladimir**  Similar mark used in shields of varying shape with or without date mid-18th to mid-19th centuries.

1763–78

1863

**Marks of purity on Russian silver from 1882**

**National mark from 1896**

**National mark 1908–17**

**National mark from 1927–58**

SPAIN

## SPAIN

From the 16th century, silver was marked with a maker's mark and a town mark. According to royal decree only silver of a purity of .930 was admissable. Date marks began to be used in certain towns at the end of the 18th century. Two lower standards were established in 1881, and silver could be assayed on request. From 1934 items were stamped with maker's mark and mark of purity.

**Barcelona** Letters BA or BAR used between early 17th and 18th centuries.

18thC

**Cordoba** Lion of varying styles, sometimes with letters COR, used between 15th and 19th centuries.

19thC

**Gerona**

1786

**Madrid**

1797

**Toledo** Letter T or TOL appears in mark from 16th century.

17thC

### Assay marks after 1881

.750  .916

## SWEDEN

By the 16th century, Swedish silver was marked with both a maker's mark and a town mark. Date letters were introduced during the late 17th century in Stockholm. During the mid-18th century the State controlled the purity of silver objects. A comprehensive date letter system was adopted throughout Sweden and Finland from 1758. From 1860 different assay offices adopted letter marks.

**Stockholm** Crown mark used from c1690 to c1715, when it was replaced by crowned head until c1850.

late 17th–early 18thC    18th/19thC

### Date letters used on Stockholm silver

| | | | | | |
|---|---|---|---|---|---|
| 1689 | A | 1713 | | 1737 | |
| 1690 | B | 1714 | | 1738 | |
| 1691 | C | 1715 | | 1739 | |
| 1692 | D | 1716 | | 1740 | |
| 1693 | E | 1717 | | 1741 | |
| 1694 | F | 1718 | | 1742 | |
| 1695 | G | 1719 | | 1743 | |
| 1696 | H | 1720 | | 1744 | |
| 1697 | I | 1721 | | 1745 | |
| 1698 | K | 1722 | | 1746 | |
| 1699 | L | 1723 | | 1747 | |
| 1700 | M | 1724 | | 1748 | |
| 1701 | N | 1725 | | 1749 | |
| 1702 | O | 1726 | | 1750 | |
| 1703 | P | 1727 | | 1751 | |
| 1704 | Q | 1728 | | 1752 | |
| 1705 | R | 1729 | | 1753 | |
| 1706 | S | 1730 | | 1754 | |
| 1707 | T | 1731 | | 1755 | |
| 1708 | U | 1732 | | 1756 | |
| 1709 | V | 1733 | | 1757 | |
| 1710 | X | 1734 | | 1758 | |
| 1711 | Y | 1735 | | | |
| 1712 | Z | 1736 | | | |

The date letters for 1713–1736 and 1737–1758 are shown as script/italic letterforms.

## Kalmar

18thC

## Malmö

18thC

## Örebro

18thC        19thC

### City marks from 1912

From 1912 the town's initial letter was used.

Ahus &#x1D538;    Gafle &#x24BC;    Karlstad &#x24B8;    Malmö &#x24C2;

Nora &#x24C3;    Sala &#x24C8;    Ystad &#x24CE; &#x1D51B;

## Date letters

### A–Z 1759–82

| | | | | | |
|---|---|---|---|---|---|
| A | 1759 | Q2 | 1798 | F4 | 1836 |
| B | 1760 | R2 | 1799 | G4 | 1837 |
| C | 1761 | S2 | 1800 | H4 | 1838 |
| D | 1762 | T2 | 1801 | I4 | 1839 |
| E | 1763 | U2 | 1802 | K4 | 1840 |
| F | 1764 | V2 | 1803 | L4 | 1841 |
| G | 1765 | X2 | 1804 | M4 | 1842 |
| H | 1766 | Y2 | 1805 | N4 | 1843 |
| I | 1767 | Z2 | 1806 | O4 | 1844 |
| K | 1768 | | | P4 | 1845 |
| L | 1769 | **A3–Z3 1807–30** | | Q4 | 1846 |
| M | 1770 | A3 | 1807 | R4 | 1847 |
| N | 1771 | B3 | 1808 | S4 | 1848 |
| O | 1772 | C3 | 1809 | T4 | 1849 |
| P | 1773 | D3 | 1810 | U4 | 1850 |
| Q | 1774 | E3 | 1811 | V4 | 1851 |
| R | 1775 | F3 | 1812 | X4 | 1852 |
| S | 1776 | G3 | 1813 | Y4 | 1853 |
| T | 1777 | H3 | 1814 | Z4 | 1854 |
| U | 1778 | I3 | 1815 | | |
| V | 1779 | K3 | 1816 | **A5–Z5 1855–78** | |
| X | 1780 | L3 | 1817 | A5 | 1855 |
| Y | 1781 | M3 | 1818 | B5 | 1856 |
| Z | 1782 | N3 | 1819 | C5D | 1857 |
| | | O3 | 1820 | 5 | 1858 |
| **A2–Z2 1783–1806** | | P3 | 1821 | E5 | 1859 |
| A2 | 1783 | Q3 | 1822 | F5G | 1860 |
| B2 | 1784 | R3 | 1823 | 5 | 1861 |
| C2 | 1785 | S3 | 1824 | H5 | 1862 |
| D2 | 1786 | T3 | 1825 | I5 | 1863 |
| E2 | 1787 | U3 | 1826 | K5 | 1864 |
| F2 | 1788 | V3 | 1827 | L5M | 1865 |
| G2 | 1789 | X3 | 1828 | 5N5 | 1866 |
| H2 | 1790 | Y3 | 1829 | O5P | 1867 |
| I2 | 1791 | Z3 | 1830 | 5Q5 | 1868 |
| K2 | 1792 | | | R5 | 1869 |
| L2 | 1793 | **A4–Z4 1831–54** | | S5 | 1870 |
| M2 | 1794 | A4 | 1831 | T5 | 1871 |
| N2 | 1795 | B4 | 1832 | U5 | 1872 |
| O2 | 1796 | C4 | 1833 | V5 | 1873 |
| P2 | 1797 | D4 | 1834 | | 1874 |
| | | E4 | 1835 | | 1875 |

| | | | | | |
|---|---|---|---|---|---|
| X5 | 1876 | F7 | 1908 | Q8 | 1942 |
| Y5 | 1877 | G7 | 1909 | R8 | 1943 |
| Z5 | 1878 | H7 | 1910 | S8 | 1944 |
| **A6–Z6 1879–1902** | | I7 | 1911 | T8 | 1945 |
| | | K7 | 1912 | U8 | 1946 |
| A6 | 1879 | L7 | 1913 | V8 | 1947 |
| B6 | 1880 | M7 | 1914 | X8 | 1948 |
| C6 | 1881 | N7 | 1915 | Y8 | 1949 |
| D6 | 1882 | O7 | 1916 | Z8 | 1950 |
| E6 | 1883 | P7 | 1917 | | |
| F6 | 1884 | Q7 | 1918 | **A9–Z9 1951–74** | |
| G6 | 1885 | R7 | 1919 | A9 | 1951 |
| H6 | 1886 | S7 | 1920 | B9 | 1952 |
| I6 | 1887 | T7 | 1921 | C9 | 1953 |
| K6 | 1888 | U7 | 1922 | D9 | 1954 |
| L6 | 1889 | V7 | 1923 | E9 | 1955 |
| M6 | 1890 | X7 | 1924 | F9 | 1956 |
| N6 | 1891 | Y7 | 1925 | G9 | 1957 |
| O6 | 1892 | Z7 | 1926 | H9 | 1958 |
| P6 | 1893 | **A8–Z8 1927–50** | | I9 | 1959 |
| Q6 | 1894 | | | K9 | 1960 |
| R6 | 1895 | A8 | 1927 | L9 | 1961 |
| S6 | 1896 | B8 | 1928 | M9 | 1962 |
| T6 | 1897 | C8 | 1929 | N9 | 1963 |
| U6 | 1898 | D8 | 1930 | O9 | 1964 |
| V6 | 1899 | E8 | 1931 | P9 | 1965 |
| X6 | 1900 | F8 | 1932 | Q9 | 1966 |
| Y6 | 1901 | G8 | 1933 | R9 | 1967 |
| Z6 | 1902 | H8 | 1934 | S9 | 1968 |
| | | I8 | 1935 | T9 | 1969 |
| **A7–Z7 1903–26** | | K8 | 1936 | U9 | 1970 |
| A7 | 1903 | L8 | 1937 | V9 | 1971 |
| B7 | 1904 | M8 | 1938 | X9 | 1972 |
| C7 | 1905 | N8 | 1939 | Y9 | 1973 |
| D7 | 1906 | O8 | 1940 | Z9 | 1974 |
| E7 | 1907 | P8 | 1941 | | |

## SWITZERLAND

The standards of purity were regulated in Zurich, Lucerne and Basel from the mid-16th century. Each canton adopted its own mark, usually a pictorial symbol with or without an intitial. Uniform purity in five standards – .935, .925, .900, .875 and 800 – was adopted from 1848. Uniform marks were adopted from 1882.

**Geneva** Similar mark used 17th to late 18th centuries.

17thC   1770    19thC

**SWITZERLAND**

### Lausanne

18thC

### Lucerne   Similar mark with shield of varying shape used from c1630 to c1760.

1701      1750

### Neuville   Similar mark with varying shield shape used between the late 16th and late 18th centuries.

1730      1752

### Vevey   Similar mark with variations used between 16th and 18th centuries.

18thC

### Zurich   Letter Z in shield used between the 16th and 18th centuries.

18thC

### Marks used 1882–1934

large .875      .800

# AMERICAN & CANADIAN HALLMARKING

American makers marked their wares with their name or initials (see pp163–165) but there was no uniform regulation of silver purity, nor any comprehensive system of date or town marking. Although American marks are scant, cities such as New York and Boston had official societies, similar to the system of guilds which presided over European silversmiths; occasionally the place of origin is marked in full alongside the maker's mark.

Modern silver produced in the USA should be marked with the maker's name and numbers indicating the purity. The word STERLING appears on silver of .925 purity.

From 1700–63, when Canada was under French rule, marks were similar to those used in France. Makers used their initials with a fleur-de-lys or crown, or star. The word MONTREAL or QUEBEC was sometimes marked on pieces made in these provinces. H or HX or XNS may be seen on pieces made in Halifax, Nova Scotia, and ST J or NB for St John, New Brunswick. From c1800 Canadian marks copied those used in England. After 1898 date letters followed the London sequence. Modern Canadian-made silver of .925 purity may be marked with the national mark – a lion's head inside a letter C.

**Canadian date letters**

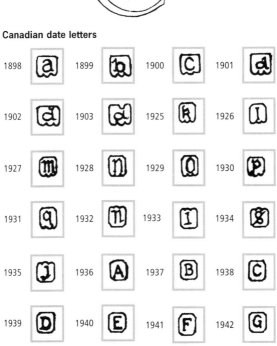

| | | | |
|---|---|---|---|
| 1898 | 1899 | 1900 | 1901 |
| 1902 | 1903 | 1925 | 1926 |
| 1927 | 1928 | 1929 | 1930 |
| 1931 | 1932 | 1933 | 1934 |
| 1935 | 1936 | 1937 | 1938 |
| 1939 | 1940 | 1941 | 1942 |
| 1943 | | | |

**Imitations of English marks**

   late 18thC

# METHODS OF
# MANUFACTURE & DECORATION

**Manufacture**  Wrought silver can be produced in one of three ways: casting, rolling or raising. Casting or moulding involves the pouring of molten silver into sand moulds. The process was used mainly for the production of candlesticks. Cuttlefish moulds were sometimes used for the casting of jewellry and smaller silver objects. In the rolling process, an ingot of silver is beaten into sheet form, rolled into cylinders and the edges seamed together to create a tube. By letting in a base, simple cups and vessels can be made. With increasing sophistication the process became used for more elaborate hollow wares. Some pieces, such as candlesticks, required strengthening or stabilizing and were often 'loaded' or 'filled'. This process, which involved fixing an iron rod inside the body using pitch or plaster, had the advantage of being significantly cheaper than casting. With raising, the metal was beaten out with a hammer, a hardening process called annealing. The piece was then heated to realign the structure of the atoms, thus restoring it to a state to withstand more beating, and so on, until the required shape was achieved.

**Decoration**  The methods of decorating silver fall into three broad types: cast and applied, repoussé and engraved.

## CAST & APPLIED DECORATION

Applied decoration refers to any decoration made separately and added, rather than integral to the form, and includes beading (a decorative border of tight beads) and a gadroon border as shown below.

Pomegranate Tureen c1811

## Strapwork decoration

Strapwork, probably brought to England by Huguenot craftsmen, consisted of interlacing straps or bands of ornament. These were originally engraved but, by the end of the 17th century, were cast and applied in a more elaborate form.

## Cut-card decoration

During the late 17th century, a more sophisticated version of strapwork, known as cut-card work whereby formalized leaves were applied to the surface in a decorative pattern, became fashionable. In much the same way as a pastry cook decorates a pie, so the silversmith cut straps and other shapes from silver and applied

Cut-card decoration

them with heat. As the period progressed, these too became chased and further decorated.

## REPOUSSE DECORATION

Repoussé means 'pushed out', and is a combination of chasing and embossing and involves chasing the embossed metal in order to refine the design.

## Chasing

A form of decoration worked with a hammer and punches, without cutting or carving the metal. Some examples of chasing are so fine they may be mistaken for engraving, of which chasing is almost the exact opposite. Chasing in high relief was popular during the late 17th century but its popularity subsided when plainer silver became fashionable during the early-

detail

18th century. However, the vogue for chased silver returned to great heights during the rococo period.

Chased decoration

### Flat chasing

Flat-chased decoration

A variation of the chasing process whereby the decoration appears in low relief. Flat chasing is worked from the front using hammers and punches, resulting in very shallow patterns similar in effect to engraving. The technique is best exemplified in early chinoiserie style silverwares.

### Embossing

Embossing is a form of relief decoration worked into the

Embossed decoration

silver with a hammer or punch, leaving a raised pattern. Embossing can be done in two ways. The craftsman may work from the inside out, resting the piece on a sandbag (a leather pillow filled with sand), which is pliant enough to withstand the shape he is creating but firm enough to maintain the form. Alternatively, the piece may be worked in reverse, the inside being

filled with pitch, which again is sufficiently pliant to allow indentation without the piece collapsing entirely. Because of the way the design is created, embossed patterns are visible on the reverse of the piece. Once the general decoration has been created, details are applied, such as the veins of a leaf or fur of an animal. This is also a type of embossing, in that a hammer and punch are used and the effect, like chasing, is visible on the reverse.

### ENGRAVING

Engraved decoration is incised into the surface of the metal. Coats-of-arms, presentation inscriptions and other marks of ownership were engraved on silverware entirely by hand, without using a hammer. Engraving is not visible on the reverse.

Engraved decoration

### Bright-cut engraving

Bright-cut decoration

A type of decorative effect achieved by engraving a faceted design that stands out sharply. It was particularly popular during the late 18th and early 19th centuries. The method is very effective when used to create ribbons and bands of swags and festoons. Bright-cut work remained fashionable until well into the 19th century; Hester Bateman (see p107) was one of its best known exponents.

## SURFACE TREATMENTS

### Planishing (hammering)

Planished decoration

A significant feature of Arts and Crafts silver is the hand-beaten or planished surface, an effect not fashionable before that period. When a piece is raised, it is beaten with a hammer while being held against an anvil or fixed 'head'. The first series of hammerings are applied with an implement of a certain convex surface and, as work continues, hammers with a progressively lesser degree of convexity are used, until the final surface, which shows no dents, is achieved with a virtually flat hammer. Halfway through this process, therefore, the surface has the dappled effect visible on the inside of many mid-18th-century coffee pots, mugs

and tankards of baluster form. The effect appealed to exponents of the Arts and Crafts movement, who perfected the difficult art of planishing a piece to a satisfactory degree of regularity.

### Pouncing
This method involves the hammering of the surface of a piece with a punch, giving a dulled texture, yet with a sparkly effect. The surface then acted as a background to other decoration.

## SILVER SUBSTITUTES

### Electroplating
This technique involved the application of a layer of pure silver to a base metal (initially copper and nickel silver, later Britannia metal) using electrolysis. The method was developed as a commercial venture by George Elkington in Birmingham in c1840 and its introduction coincided with a fashion for naturalistic designs not easily produced by other methods. EPBM and EPNS indicate electroplated Britannia metal and electroplated nickel silver respectively. A large amount of serviceable silverwares was produced using both materials and, although widely used today, neither is particularly collectable in their own right.

### Electrotyping
Electrotyping is a sophisticated development of electroplating that facilitates the accurate imitation of solid objects. A plaster mould is taken of the original object, coated with plumbago (graphite), then subjected to electrolysis. The silver deposited evenly on the plumbago provides an exact imitation of the original mould. Like electroplating, electrotyping was introduced by Elkington & Co.

### Close plating
A method of applying a layer of silver foil to steel, an early decorative process used by cutlers to protect steel knives (especially dessert knives) from staining.

### Gilding
A method of applying a thin layer of gold to silver: mixture of gold leaf and mercury was spread over relevant area and heated until the mercury porated. Following the introduction of electroplating, ilding, which produced toxic mercury fumes, tlawed.

## Armorials and Cartouches

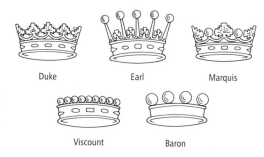

Duke          Earl          Marquis

Viscount          Baron

Since pride of ownership first began, people have
inscribed their silver within a decorative frame or
cartouche. The humblest inscriptions may only be
initials; the grandest, coats-of-arms and crests, but the
type of shield and the style of cartouche can provide help
in dating a piece that lacks a full set of marks, and may
even indicate the original owner.

A full set of armorials can appear on larger pieces: this
comprises a coat-of-arms surrounded by a cartouche,
mantling, a motto and, for members of the peerage, a
coronet and supporters.

## Crests and Coat of Arms within Cartouches

Coat-of-Arms within
Cartouche

Crest

Crest

There is an important distinction to be made between a crest and a coat-of-arms: a single crest may be shared by anything up to 20 families, whereas a coat-of-arms is traceable to a particular family or even a particular man and wife, which adds to the interest of the piece. Crests are sometimes coupled with mottoes. English crests have the motto below, whereas Scottish crests have the motto over the top.

Coats-of-arms are a good guide to dating. They are also used in Continental Europe in styles that correspond to the English styles of each period. German arms often include helmets.

### Inscriptions

Birmingham 1895

Inscriptions that are contemporary with the piece may add to its value. The most desirable are those that have a naval or military content, or are connected with institutions such as Lloyd's Bank or the East India Company. Those that include the name of well-known people are also desirable. However, religious inscriptions (and items intended for religious, rather than for secular use) are not currently in great demand.

Inscriptions to civil engineers were common in the Victorian period.

### Initials

London 1720

Some pieces, particularly earlier ones, are engraved with three initials in a triangle. The upper, single initial usually represents that of the family surname, the lower two being the initials of the forenames of the husband and wife. Pieces thus engraved were often given as wedding presents. Initials can be helpful in tracing a coat-of-arms or a crest to a particular family or person.

### Replacement and erasure of arms

When silver changed hands, the new owners sometimes erased the existing coat-of-arms and replaced it with their own, an act which can reduce the value of a piece (see Fakes & Alterations pp172–179).

## BORDERS

Borders are an important decorative element of many different types of silverware. Their changing styles can give a useful indication of the date of an object. At the beginning of the 18th century, simple moulded borders were applied to wares. Elaborately scrolled borders were sometimes pierced and often further embellished with cast and applied motifs; shells were especially prevalent. During the latter half of the 18th century borders became more simple and delicate. Heavier borders were favoured during the Regency period; gadroon borders were particularly popular at this time. Throughout the 19th century the borders of most earlier periods were resurrected, although their proportion in relation to the overall size of the piece was often increased.

Shell and Scroll Border

Detail of above

Bath border

Beaded border

Shell and Gadroon border

# SILVER STYLES

Style can prove a particularly useful guide to dating silver; recognizable shapes offer an immediate indication of the origin and period of a piece. The majority of collectable silver available to us today dates from the mid-17th century and later. Earlier pieces rarely exist outside museums or churches and do not really concern us within this book. The earliest silver that most collectors are likely to encounter is Commonwealth silver (c1655–60), which was usually extremely plain and of basic construction.

In reaction to the austerity of the Cromwellian era, the Restoration saw a revival in the popularity of display silver and an explosion of variety in design. King Charles II, returning from exile, brought with him Continental craftsmen whose new styles and manufacturing techniques altered the appearance of British silver. Fluid foliate shapes were used to decorate silverwares, and floral motifs and fruit were popular adornments.

The Revocation of the Edict of Nantes in 1685 brought thousands of French Protestants, or Huguenots, to Britain. Among them were many superb silversmiths with their own approach to manufacture and decoration. The raising of the silver standard in 1697 (see pp8 – 9) brought further changes in style. Huguenot silversmiths were used to working with metal of this standard and British silver styles fell heavily under their influence at this time. The Huguenots are particularly associated with lavishly ornamented silver and embellished their wares with engraved decoration derived from French pattern books; hitherto engraving had been little used by English silversmiths. The French craftsmen also introduced new items such as ewers, basins and tureens which, until this date, were not in general use in Britain.

Silver dating from the period during and after the reign of Queen Anne (1702–14) was plainer in shape and form. Vessels were generally straight-sided, cylindrical and tapering, below high domed tops; octagonal shapes were popular from c1710. As tea, coffee and chocolate became fashionable drinks, teapots, coffee pots and chocolate pots became increasingly popular. Sauce boats, snuff boxes and racing cups were also first made during this period.

Throughout the 18th century silverware was made both plain and fancy. The culvilinear lines of the period up to the 1770s were the basis for the elaborate and exuberant rococo decoration on the most expensive pieces; in the same way the post 1770s classical shapes re the vehicles for the cast and applied decorative ifs in the ancient style. Rococo came to England from pe, particularly through France, and was promoted h influential Huguenot silversmiths as Pierre Platel ul de Lamerie.

Designs for high-style pieces often incorporated fanciful Chinese and Gothic decoration. Handles in the shape of a 'C' scroll, shell motifs, and sinuous foliage are typical of rococo, which reached the height of its popularity in the 1730s and '40s. Pieces with extreme rococo decoration are rare and expensive, but simpler wares of the period usually contain minor elements of the style.

Classicism became fashionable during the last quarter of the 18th century, replacing rococo entirely by the 1780s. It was inspired by growing interest in Greco-Roman art and architecture, following the excavations of Herculaneum and Pompeii, and was popularized in the designs of architect Robert Adam. Adam is known also to have worked closely with Boulton and Fothergill of Birmingham to design 'Adam' silverware. During the classical period, heavy gadroon edges were replaced with beading, and swirling tendrils became carefully tailored drapes. The emphasis was on grace, elegance and simplicity. Silver of this period often mirrors the oval shapes of Greek and Roman vases. Decorative motifs drawn from classical antiquity include swags, rams' heads, laurel leaves and acanthus leaves, and are delicately refined. By the 1790s, silver surfaces were often engraved in a new style known as 'bright cut' (see p84).

Towards the end of the 18th century, a new style evolved based on increased knowledge and understanding of Greek, Roman and Egyptian antiquity. In England it is known as 'Regency', in France it is termed 'Empire'. During this period, which lasted from c1790–1830, the proportions of silverwares changed dramatically, often becoming massively heavy. Decorative motifs included lyres, lions' feet, masks and thick and fleshy foliage.

The French revival, which resurrected the naturalistic curvilinear forms of the rococo period, started in c1827 and continued after the death of George IV in 1830. The rococo revival mingled the foliate forms of the early 18th century with the larger proportions of Regency style. Silverwares are often broad and low, with a strong horizontal emphasis and boldly applied decoration. The Gothic motifs which had provided an undercurrent of inspiration throughout much of the 18th century, found great favour with the sombre Victorian outlook, and is reflected in silverwares by decorative Gothic arches, pinnacles and spires decorated with crockets.

The Great Exhibition of 1851 revolutionized public access to domestic items in a fashionable style; new machinery and materials facilitated the mass manufactur of exotic-looking pieces for a modest price. By the end the 19th century, domestic silver was produced on a scale, whilst electroplated nickel silver and electropla Britannia metal fashioned in silver shapes had found

Silver card case, by David Pettifer, embossed with Crystal Palace, Birmingham 1850

market in their own right. As the Middle and Far East caught the imagination of the English, Moorish and Islamic patterns were incorporated into those already existing, and it is not surprising that a movement should emerge in support of traditional hand crafting. Under the influence of the Arts and Crafts movement of the late 19th century, designs, particularly for furniture and silver, became sinuous and natural. It was also at this time that octagonal-sided wares, in true reproduction of the early 18th-century style, became fashionable once again. Indeed, during the first 30 years of the 20th century, all earlier styles were faithfully reproduced and, apart from the severe undecorated lines of the Art Deco style, there was generally little innovation in styles from that period.

Because of Ireland's political connections, Irish silver has, for the most part, had strong links with contemporary silver in England. Some exquisite early Celtic silver survives in Ireland, from between the 8th and 12th centuries. There is then a gap of four centuries, until the re-establishment of the Dublin Goldsmiths' Company. Until c1720, Irish silver is similar in style to London silver, but remained largely unaffected by the French Huguenot influence. During the 18th century, Ireland's largely absentee Anglo-Irish aristocracy tended to buy silver in London and to demand that any Irish-bought silver exhibit English characteristics. It was only with the development of a more purely Irish middle class that Irish silver was able to develop its own shapes.

Irish silver is sometimes of a lower quality than English silver, but frequently exhibits exquisite bright-cut work and unusual features, such as pointed handles. Ireland's Union with England introduced the English to the rich surface decoration popular in Ireland; this was a style that found an admiring audience in Regency and Victorian England. Though initially good for Ireland's flourishing silver trade, the Union ultimately destroyed it, as the Irish styles began to be copied in England. However, from the beginning of the 20th century a national style re-emerged, based on the historic Celtic forms that regained popularity after a Gaelic revival.

# ILLUSTRATED SILVER STYLES

## Cake baskets

Most baskets incorporate pierced decoration which can be vulnerable to damage; condition is therefore important in assessing value. Few predate the mid-18th century. Early baskets are usually oval, some have side handles. Later ones are usually lighter in weight and have 'swing' handles. Oblong and circular shaped baskets were made from the end of the 18th century. Hallmarks are usually found on the base, footrim or side.

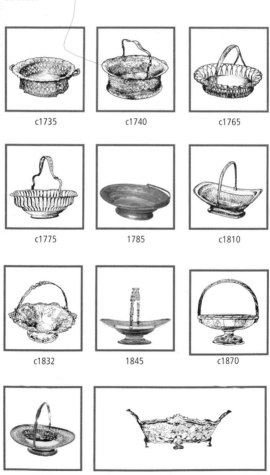

c1735

c1740

c1765

c1775

1785

c1810

c1832

1845

c1870

1911

Netherlands, c1775

## Candelabra

Most candelabra date from the mid 18th century and the design of the bases follows that of candlesticks of the same period. Candelabra are rarer and considerably more sought-after than candlesticks. Most are hallmarked on the base and the branches should also be marked.

1843

Late 19thC

France, c1788

## Candlesticks

Candlesticks became taller and heavier throughout the 18th century, ranging from about 6in (15cm) to 11in (30cm). Hallmarks are most commonly found on the underside of the base of cast sticks, or on the side of the base of loaded ones; detachable sconces and nozzles should also be marked. Candlesticks nearly always come in pairs or large sets and fall considerably in value when sold singly.

1702    1726    1743

1764    1790    c1850

## Casters

Casters were used from the late 17th century onwards, usually for dispensing sugar or pepper. Early examples have straight sides and pierced covers; later in the century, octagonal and baluster shapes were introduced and some covers were unpierced (blind). Casters became taller throughout the 18th century. Most are hallmarked on the base or on the side; detachable covers should also be marked.

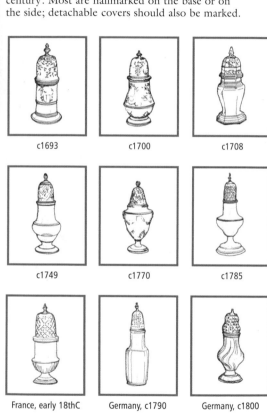

c1693

c1700

c1708

c1749

c1770

c1785

France, early 18thC

Germany, c1790

Germany, c1800

1693

c1800

1714

## Coffee & chocolate pots

Most coffee pots date from the early 18th century.
Early coffee pots have side handles and a tapering
cylindrical shape with high domed lids. Later in the
century lids were shallower, and baluster, vase-shaped,
and oblong pots were popular. Marks should be
scattered on the base or in a line on the side.

1741           1742           1784

1798           1824           1881

1724

## Cruets

Spices and flavourings were an important element
in 18th-century cooking and cruet frames, to contain
the necessary bottles and casters on the table, became
prevalent during the century. Cruets are very varied
in form; many contain silver-mounted glass bottles.
They are usually marked on the main stand as well
as on the component parts.

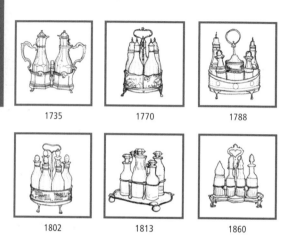

1735          1770          1788

1802          1813          1860

c1806

## Entrée dishes

Entrée dishes became popular from the 1770s onwards. Until the 1830s most were oval or rectangular in shape. Earlier examples are often shallower than those made during the Regency period and later. Handles are usually detachable. Entrée dishes were made in sets of two or more and marked with numbers or dots to identify their matching lid. Hallmarks are usually in a straight line on the lid and base.

c1890

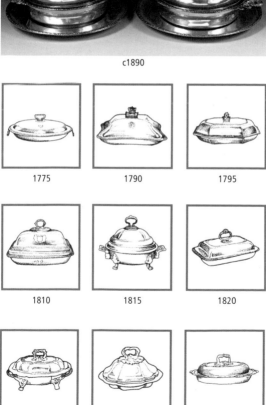

1775

1790

1795

1810

1815

1820

1830

1835

1845

## Epergnes & centrepieces

Epergnes were used from the middle of the 18th
century to display fruit and sweetmeats on the table.
Early examples consist of a large basket surrounded
by four smaller containers or baskets. Later designs
can have six or more baskets; most are highly elaborate.
All the component parts of the épergnes and
centrepieces should be marked.

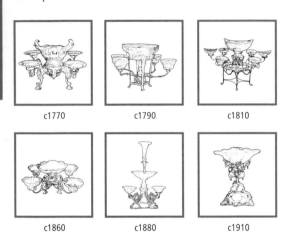

c1770          c1790          c1810

c1860          c1880          c1910

## Milk & cream jugs

Small jugs for milk or cream were uncommon during
the early 18th century and usually resemble coffee pots
of the period, with high domed lids. During the 1720s,
small jugs without lids were introduced. Mid-18th-
century examples had three cast feet, scrolled handles
and curvilinear rims. Later, plain pear-shapes with
pedestal feet predominate. Jugs are usually marked on
the underneath or on the body by the handle or spout.

1729          1730          1739

1745

1756

1765

1795

1800

1840

1830

SALTS

## Salts

Salt was kept in pairs of salt cellars from the beginning of the 18th century. Trencher salts were among the earliest examples and are usually marked inside the bowl. By the middle of the century most salts had three feet, sometimes decorated with a lion's-head mask. During the neo-classical period oval salts with pedestal bases were made. Salts are most usually marked on the base; on circular shapes the marks will be scattered.

c1592

c1594

1650–1700

c1695

c1760

c1761

c1790

c1840

c1850

c1850

c1855

c1870

## Salvers & waiters

Early salvers are often circular in shape with a central foot. Armorials were usually the only surface decoration before 1730. From c1730 onwards square shapes, increasingly elaborate borders and surface decoration proliferated and some salvers had three or four feet. Oval shapes were popular from c1785.

Salvers measuring under 6in (15cm) are termed waiters. Hallmarks are usually found on the surface of the tray before c1720, or on the underside after that date.

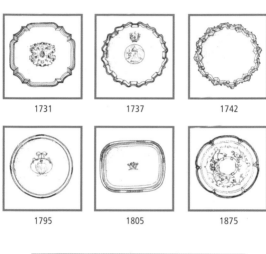

1731          1737          1742

1795          1805          1875

1765

### Sauce boats

The earliest sauce boats date from c1715. Early examples are shallow with two handles, lips and a wavy rim. From c1730 sauce boats became deeper with a single lip and central pedestal foot. Later examples often had three feet. Hallmarks are usually underneath in a straight line.

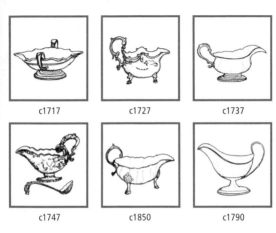

c1717          c1727          c1737

c1747          c1850          c1790

### Spoons

Early spoons had fig-shaped bowls and decorative finials, sometimes modelled in the form of an apostle. By the 1680s the bowl became more ovoid with a rat-tail rib at the back, and handles terminated in a trefid. During the Queen Anne period the handles evolved in the dog's nose form. Throughout the 18th century, the bowl became more pointed and the Hanoverian (sometimes called Rat-tail) and Old English patterns predominated for handles. During the 19th century, many new, sometimes highly elaborate, patterns were introduced, most of which continue to be made today.

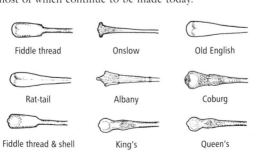

Fiddle thread          Onslow          Old English

Rat-tail          Albany          Coburg

Fiddle thread & shell          King's          Queen's

Trefid spoon, c1790

A selection of apostle spoons: St John, St Peter, St Bartholomew,
St Andrew, St Thomas, St Paul

## Tankards

Most tankards date from c1660 to the late 18th century.
Tankards differ from mugs in that they have lids,
although they follow a similar stylistic development.
Early examples are usually straight-sided; during the
late 17th century chased decoration, cut-card work
and engraving were often used to embellish surfaces.
Tankards of the 18th century are usually plain, possibly
only ornamented with a coat-of-arms. Marks should be
found on the side of the body or base and on the lid.

c1670            c1701            c1728

c1731            c1776            c1795

### Teapots

Teapots were made from the early 18th century onwards. Until c1760 they are relatively small because tea was expensive. The early pear-shaped form was replaced from c1730–50 by the bullet shape. From c1770 drum-shaped and then oval teapots became fashionable. The oblong shape was introduced in the early 19th century. Marks are usually found on the base; lids should also be marked.

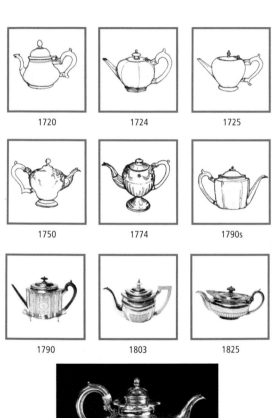

1720     1724     1725

1750     1774     1790s

1790     1803     1825

1849

## Tureens

Sauce tureens first appeared c1760. Most have covers
with a cut-out to accommodate the sauce ladle;
some also have trays on which they stand. During the
Adam period sauce tureens were decorated with beaded
borders and classical motifs and have pedestal feet.
Some later examples have four legs and were more
heavily proportioned. Few sauce tureens were made
after 1830. Marks are usually found on the underneath
of the body and on the lid.

1776          1790          1811

1840       France, 1805       Russia, 1811

## Two-handled cups

Early two-handled cups are termed caudle cups or
porringers. Caudle was a drink traditionally given to
women after childbirth. Most have covers and are of a
straight-sided or bulbous shape. From the 18th century,
two-handled cups were used at banquets and as
decorative pieces, becoming taller with a pedestal foot.
During the 19th century the two-handled cup was a
popular shape for trophies; some were of large
proportions and lavishly ornamented. Marks should be
found on the base, body or handle and on the lid.

c1692

c1714

c1776

## Continental Cups

Netherlands, late 16thC

Germany, c1600

Netherlands, c1642

Germany, c1750

Germany, c1890

## Wine Funnels

Wine funnels were made from c1770 and used for decanting wine. They usually consist of either a conical bowl with a detachable spout, or a main bowl containing a liner with a perforated base. A piece of muslin was inserted in the base to strain the wine. Most were plain as they were purely functional objects. Complete hallmarks should be found on the bowl and the spout, and the inner bowl should also have marks.

1710

1790

1800

1799

1827

# IMPORTANT BRITISH MAKERS

Among silversmiths there are a few names that stand out as being responsible for a consistently high standard of design and craftsmanship.

### Charles Robert Ashbee (1863–1942)

An influential designer of early 20th-century silver, Ashbee trained as an architect before becoming a leader of the Arts and Craft movement. He was a founder member of the Guild of Handicraft, which consisted of a circle of artist-craftsmen who sought to perpetuate medieval hand-craftsmanship. Charles Ashbee had no formal training as a silversmith but his early work was especially innovative. In 1909 Ashbee published *Modern English Silverwork* in which he expounded his theories on silver design.

### Asprey & Co Ltd (c1781–present day)

The company is believed to have been founded in 1781 in Mitcham, Surrey by William Asprey. By 1805, the firm had moved to London premises and was under the direction of Francis Kennedy. Early in the 19th century Kennedy was joined by Charles Asprey Snr who, by the middle of the century, had left Kennedy and set up his own premises in New Bond Street. Throughout the 19th century and afterwards Asprey was acclaimed as one of London's leading silver manufacturers and retailers.

### Hester Bateman (1709–94)

Hester Needham married John Bateman, a maker of gold watch chains, in 1732, and established a family silversmith business near the City of London. Early pieces were mainly flatwares but they later graduated to larger domestic objects and produced vast quantities of attractive silverwares. Hester Bateman first registered her own maker's mark in 1761, a year after her husband's death. However, her mark is rarely found on pieces dated earlier than 1774 because during the intervening years she was occupied running the shop and co-ordinating commissions. After 1774 she appears to have concentrated on her own silversmithing, producing refined shapes with restrained decoration, often restricted to beading along the edges. Much of Hester

Bateman's work was commissioned by other contemporary silversmiths, many of whom obliterated her mark and replaced it with their own. On her retirement in 1790, Bateman handed over the business to her sons, Peter and Jonathan. On Jonathan's death in 1791, his widow Ann entered a mark in conjunction with her brother-in-law. Her son, William, joined the partnership in 1800 and the three entered a joint mark. The mark of Peter and William Bateman was entered on Ann's retirement in 1805. Peter remained in control of the business until 1839, when he handed it down to his son, William (see also p116).

### John Cafe (active 1740–57)

Little is known of John Cafe (or possibly Case), other than that he registered his mark with Goldsmiths in 1742 and specialized in the manufacture of candlesticks, chambersticks, snuffers and trays. His business was bankrupt in 1757 and was taken over by his brother William (see also p119).

### The Courtauld family (active 1708–1807)

A prolific maker of domestic pieces, Augustine Courtauld was apprenticed to Simon Pantin in 1701 and registered his first mark in 1708. Samuel Courtauld (b1720), the son of Augustine, married Louisa Perina Ogier in 1747. Little of his strongly rococo-style work survives. Louisa took over the family business on her husband's death in 1765. Her son Samuel also joined the firm and later emigrated to America (see pp121–122).

### Christopher Dresser (1834–1904)

An important English designer and writer who was preoccupied with the need for good design and the importance of mechanization, Christopher Dresser designed revolutionary modern-style silverwares and electroplate for the firms of Elkington and Hukin & Heath from 1875 to 1878. His designs are usually dictated by the function of the object, most are extremely simple and geometric in appearance; exposed rivets are a favourite motif.

### Elkington & Co (1801–65)

Elkington & Co are renowned for their development of the electroplate process which revolutionized the production of inexpensive silverware. The technique was first patented by the company in 1840. Later Elkington granted special licences to other companies, such as the French firm Christofle, to produce their own electroplate. Elkington produced large quantities of useful household objects, many of which were used to equip hotels and clubs. Designs reflect a great variety of influences; Eastern and Italian Renaissance motifs were used frequently.

###  Andrew Fogelberg (1732–93)

Andrew Fogelberg came from Sweden and was probably already trained when he arrived in London c1770. He formed a partnership with Stephen Gilbert, working with him from 1780 to 1793 (see p127), and is especially well known for pieces in the popular neo-classical style. Fogelberg seems to have pioneered the application of decorative cameo-like medallions to his silverwares. Paul Storr (see p112) was apprenticed to Fogelberg.

###  Robert Garrard (active 1818)

In 1792, Robert Garrard joined the partnership established by George Wickes and Edward Wakelin (see p112 and p151), which then became known as Wakelin & Garrard. Wakelin passed the business to Garrard when he retired in 1802, and he in turn was succeeded by his three sons Robert (1793–1881), James and Sebastian. The firm remained in Garrard's hands and became the Crown Jewellers and Goldsmiths in 1830.

###  Eliza Godfrey (active 1741)

Eliza Godfrey was the most prolific and popular of the women silversmiths operating in the mid-18th century. Godfrey had been briefly married to Abraham Buteaux (see p119), and married Benjamin Godfrey in 1732. However, in 1741 she was left widowed by Benjamin Godfrey (see p129). Between her marriages and after her second husband's death she registered her own marks, continuing the business with enormous success and producing such fine silverwares that she was eligible for Bateman's title of 'the best woman silversmith of the 18th century'. Her work tends to feature cast and chased work with intricate pierced fretwork in the rococo style.

## The Hennell family

The Hennell family established a silvermaking dynasty in the 18th century that continues today. The first David Hennell registered his mark in 1736. He was joined by his son Robert in 1763, who worked with him until 1797. Robert Hennell registered his mark in 1753. He was a pioneer of the neo-classical style, revived in England by the work of Robert Adam. Hennell is best-known for fine small silver, sweetmeat baskets, épergnes, salt cellars and cutlery. David and Robert Hennell entered their mark in 1768. Robert and Samuel Hennell registered a mark in 1802. (see pp132–133).

## Archibald Knox (1854–1933)

Archibald Knox was born and educated on the Isle of Man. His observation of the Celtic remains there is reflected in the Celtic motifs decorating his silverwares. He made silver and other metalwares for Liberty & Co and was the most important of their designers. Archibald Knox was commissioned by Liberty to produce designs for the 'Cymric' silverware range. Among his most sought-after silverwares are those embellished with coloured enamelling.

## Paul de Lamerie (1688–1751)

A Huguenot, Paul de Lamerie was born in the Low Countries. His parents brought him to England in 1689, after the Revocation of the Edict of Nantes. He served his apprenticeship with Pierre Platel in 1703 and registered his first mark in 1712. De Lamerie worked consistently in Britannia silver until 1732, even though after 1720 it was no longer compulsory. He entered a sterling silver mark in 1732. In 1739, de Lamerie entered a third mark and moved his workshop to Gerrard Street in London where he died in 1751. Although other 18th-century silversmiths equalled de Lamerie in skill, his work is undoubtedly the most popular and collectable today. His early wares were in the restrained Queen Anne style but his most popular and famous pieces, many of which were royal commissions, are in an elaborate and highly decorative rococo style. However, de Lamerie also produced large numbers of simple and useful wares.

### Pierre Platel (active 1699–1719)

Platel was a French Huguenot silversmith who became a member of the Goldsmiths' Company in 1699. His work typifies the elaborate rococo styles favoured by the English aristocracy, for which the Huguenot silversmiths were renowned. The Prince of Wales was one of his patrons. Among his most elaborate and celebrated works are a ewer and dish in the form of a helmet made in 1701 (now at Chatsworth House). Platel had several apprentices who became successful in their own right, the most celebrated was Paul de Lamerie (see previous page).

### Omar Ramsden and Alwyn Carr (1873–1939)

Ramsden and Carr registered a joint mark in 1898. They were among the new generation of silversmiths who carried on the ideals of traditional hand-made techniques into the modern age of mass production. Ramsden entered a Gothic-style mark when he set up on his own in 1918. He was greatly influenced by Celtic art and medieval influences are often reflected in his designs. His work commonly features a hammer-marked (planished) surface (see pp81–85) and he often applied a Latin signature in addition to his mark.

### Rundell, Bridge & Rundell (1788–1842)

The firm was established by Philip Rundell (1743–1827) and became one of London's most successful makers. In 1788, Rundell formed a partnership with John Bridge (see p118) and they were joined by Edmund Waller Rundell in 1803. The company was patronized by the Royal family, and had warrants from both the Prince of Wales and Duke of York. In 1806, they were recorded as employing 1,000 workers. Many of their more important wares were made by specially commissioned independent silversmiths, such as Paul Storr and Benjamin Smith (see below). John Flaxman modelled figures for some of the enormous presentation pieces in which the company specialized. The firm also made good quality less elaborate pieces.

### Benjamin Smith (b1764)

An important Regency silversmith, Benjamin Smith was one of the major suppliers of wares to Rundell & Bridge (see previous page). Many designs were very similar to those of Paul Storr (see below); Smith specialized in baskets and open-work items. Before 1792, he formed a company known as Boulton & Smith with his brother, James, and Matthew Boulton of Birmingham. In 1801, a disagreement led to the formation of a new partnership between Boulton and James Smith. In 1802, Smith moved from Birmingham to Greenwich. He formed a partnership with Digby Scott, registering marks with him in 1802 and 1803. In 1807, Smith registered two marks alone. In partnership with James he registered another mark in 1809. Further marks were recorded in 1812, 1814, 1816 (with his son Benjamin Jnr) and 1818. Smith had a reputation for being difficult to work with (see also p118 and p147).

### Paul Storr (1771–1844)

Paul Storr is perhaps the most famous of early 19th-century silversmiths. Originally apprenticed to the Swedish-born plate worker, Andrew Fogelberg (see p109), he concentrated on the production of fine and elaborate presentation silver, some of it by royal commission. As one of the English silversmiths who interpreted the French Empire style in a less formal manner, Storr was instrumental in the development of the English Regency style. He opened his own shop in 1796. Between 1807 and 1819 he worked in association with Rundell and Bridge (see previous page), during which time he produced a wide range of wares, mainly in the ancient Roman or rococo styles. In 1822, Storr formed a partnership with John Mortimer that was to last until 1838. Unlike Paul de Lamerie, Storr appears to have made little ordinary or plain silver.

### George Wickes (1698–1761)

George Wickes was apprenticed to Simon Wastell on 2 December 1712 and registered his first two marks in 1722. Wickes had a line of distinguished clients: among his most famous commissions were the Pelham Gold Cup, made to designs by William Kent, c1736, and a table service consisting of 170 pieces, made for the Earl of Leinster. Most of his work reflects the French rococo style, with asymmetrical curvilinear decorative motifs which were popular at the time.

# BRITISH & IRISH MAKERS

Listed below is a selection of some of the other best-known British and Irish silversmiths from the 17th to the early 20th century. London was by far the most popular centre for British silversmiths; the vast majority of recorded makers were active in and around the capital. Therefore, unless otherwise stated, all the following makers may be assumed to have been London-based.

Knowledge of the working lives of most silversmiths is largely gleaned from the various assay offices and from records kept by the Worshipful Company of Silver & Goldsmiths. Before a silversmith could register a mark on his own he was obliged to serve as an apprentice to a 'Master' (a qualified silversmith). After a specified time the apprentice was granted his freedom (ie he was no longer apprenticed) and was permitted to set up business on his own. Many silversmiths went on to become members of the Company of Gold & Silversmiths, a process known as 'being clothed with the livery' or 'liveried'. Some then progressed to become part of the governing body, becoming members of court, then wardens. The head of the company was known as the Prime Warden.

All gold and silversmiths (also known as plateworkers) were basically divided into two categories: largeworkers and smallworkers. Largeworkers, as the name suggests, made objects of a more substantial size such as baskets, dishes, tureens and large hollow wares. Candlestick makers and salver makers were largeworkers. Smallworkers made small pieces such as vinaigrettes, wine labels and matchboxes. Buckle makers, snuff box makers, spectacle makers and watch-case makers were all types of smallworker.

The following list gives details of the apprenticeship of recorded makers together with the dates of their marks and examples of them and, where appropriate, the types of wares for which they are best-known. Many silversmiths registered a variety of marks.

Daniel Smith and Robert Sharp, c1763

Thomas Wallis, late 18thC

David and Robert Hennell, c1763

**William Abdy** Registered marks as a smallworker in 1763, 1767, 1769, 1779 and 1784. His son Thomas worked as his apprentice. Died 1790.

**Robert Abercromby** Marks registered in 1731, 1739 and 1740. Specialized in the making of salvers.

**Robert Abercromby & George Hindmarsh** Salver makers (see above). Registered mark in 1731.

**George W. Adams** London plateworker. Registered mark in 1840.

**Stephen Adams & William Jury** Smallworkers. Registered marks c1758 and 1759.

**Charles Aldridge** Apprenticed to his uncle, Edward Aldridge and to Edward Adle. Registered mark in partnership with Henry Green (see below) in 1775 and further marks in 1786 and 1789.

**Charles Aldridge & Henry Green** Plateworkers. Registered marks in 1775 (see above).

**Edward Aldridge** Registered marks in 1724 and 1739. Registered mark in partnership with John Stampe in 1753. In 1742 tried by the Goldsmiths' Company for counterfeiting marks but acquitted by the jury (see below).

**Edward Aldridge & John Stamper** Recorded mark in 1753 (see above and below).

**William Alexander** Apprenticed to Isabella Archer in 1707 and made a freeman in 1716. Registered only mark as a largeworker in 1743. One of the most important chandelier makers of the mid-18th century.

**Joseph Allen & Mordecai Fox** Allen recorded his first mark in partnership with Fox in 1730 from St Swithin's Lane, and his second with him in 1739.

**John Angell** Son of John Angell Snr and apprenticed to him in 1825. John Angell Snr did not register a mark but worked with his brother Joseph. John Angell Jnr registered a mark in partnership with uncle, Joseph Angell, in 1831 (see below).

**Joseph Angell** Apprenticed to Henry Nutting in 1796. Two marks registered in 1811 and 1824 (see above and below).

**George Angell & John Charles Angell** John Charles Angell went into business with his eldest son, George Angell. Marks registered in 1840 and 1844. After father's death in 1850, George continued the business under the name George Angell & Co until 1860, when further marks were registered. He died in 1884.

**Arthur Annesley** Registered mark as a largeworker in 1758.

**Peter Archambo Snr** Apprenticed to Jacob Margas. Registered marks in 1721, 1722 and 1739. Renowned for prolific output of all standard types of silverware.

**Peter Archambo Jnr & Peter Meure** Peter Archambo Jnr was a cousin of Peter Meure. Mark registered in 1750; usually found on dinner plates.

**Hugh Arnett & Edward Pocock** Arnett was apprenticed to Isaac Davenport. Arnett & Pocock registered mark in 1720.

**William Atkinson** Apprenticed to William Bellasis of the Merchant Taylors' Company in 1718 and became a freeman in 1725. Registered two marks in 1725 as a largeworker from the Golden Cup, New Fish Street Hill.

**William Bagnall** The son of a shopkeeper, apprenticed to Gabriel Sleath in 1736. Registered mark as a largeworker in 1744 from Smithfield.

**Thomas Bamford** Apprenticed to Charles Adam in 1703. Entered first two marks as a largeworker in 1720 and another in 1739 from Foster Lane. Known as a caster maker as was his master and his apprentice, Samuel Wood.

**John Barbe** Registered marks as largeworker in 1735, 1739 and 1742.

### Edward, John & William Barnard
One of the oldest surviving firms. William served apprenticeship under his father, Edward in 1815. They entered a mark together with William's brother, John, in 1829. Known as Edward Barnard & Sons from 1829–1910, and Barnard & Sons Ltd from 1910 to the present day (see below).

### Edward Barnard, Edward Barnard Jnr, John Barnard & William Barnard
Registered their mark together in 1829 as plateworkers (see above).

### Edward Barnett
Apprenticed to Antony Nelme. Registered mark as a largeworker in 1715.

### George Baskerville
Apprenticed to Joseph Sanders in c1732. Registered marks in 1738, 1745, 1751, 1755 (in partnership with William Sampel) and 1780 (see below).

### George Baskerville & William Sampel
Registered mark together in 1755 (see above).

### James Le Bass
Early 19th-century Dublin maker of ecclesiastical and table silver.

### Peter & Jonathan Bateman
Peter and Jonathan were sons of Hester Bateman (see p107). They entered a mark in 1790 and a further six marks in 1791 (see below).

### Peter & Ann Bateman
Ann married Jonathan Bateman in 1769 and on his death joined in partnership with brother-in-law Peter Bateman, registering a mark with him in 1791 (see above and below).

### Peter, Ann & William Bateman
Ann registered mark with brother-in-law Peter and son William in 1800 (see above and below).

### Peter & William Bateman
Son and grandson of Hester Bateman, registered mark in 1805 (see above and below).

### William Bateman
Born 1774, second son of Jonathan and Ann Bateman, grandson of Hester. Registered marks with Peter and Ann Bateman in 1800, with Peter only in 1805, and alone in 1815. In c1840 sold the family business.

**Samuel Bates** Marks registered in 1728 and 1744. Liveried in 1752.

 **Richard Bayley** Apprenticed to Charles Overing in 1699, and to John Gibbons in 1704. Became a freeman in 1706. Registered marks in 1708 (from Foster Lane), 1720 and 1739. He was liveried in 1712. His son Richard Bayley was apprenticed to Samuel Spindler. Best known for his simple and useful domestic wares.

 **Richard Beale** London largeworker. Apprenticed to Jonathan Newton in 1722 and John le Sage in 1725. Three marks are recorded, in 1733, 1739 and 1746.

 **George Beale** London plateworker whose first recorded mark dates from 1699 and second from 1713.

 **Joseph Bell** Apprenticed to Robert Timbrel, later worked in partnership with him. Recorded mark dates from 1716.

 **William Bell** Apprenticed to William Burton in 1748. Marks registered in 1759, 1763, 1769, 1772, 1774 and 1777.

 **Edward Bennett** Apprenticed to Henry Miller in 1720 and Samuel Hutton in 1725. Marks recorded in 1727, 1731, 1737, 1739 and 1747. Liveried in 1737.

 **John Berthellot** Marks registered in 1738, 1739, 1746 and 1750.

 **John Bettridge** Mid-19th century Birmingham silversmith, best known for snuff boxes and other small wares.

 **Jonathan Bignell** Largeworker. Registered marks in 1718 and 1720.

 **Samuel Blackborrow** Apprenticed to William Fawdery. Marks recorded in 1719 and 1721.

 **Cornelius Bland** Served apprenticeship under James Bishop, entered marks in 1772 and 1788. Thomas Young served as his apprentice in 1779 (see p118).

**BRITISH & IRISH MAKERS**

 **James & Elizabeth Bland** Elizabeth was the widow of Cornelius. Registered mark in partnership with son James in 1794 (see previous page).

 **William Bond & John Phipps** Largeworkers. A mark was recorded in 1754.

 **Thomas Bolton** Prominent early 18th-century maker of ecclesiastical silverware, based in Dublin.

 **George Boothby** Largeworker. Marks registered in 1720 and 1739. Recorded as working from The Parrot in the Strand, hence the parrot in mark.

 **Matthew Boulton** Important Birmingham-based manufacturer. Formed partnership with John Fothergill 1762–82. Boulton was active in establishing the Birmingham Assay Office. Prior to 1773, when the Birmingham office opened, his silver was marked with Chester mark. Boulton died in 1809 but his manufactory continued throughout the 19th century.

 **Thomas Bradbury & Sons** Sheffield plate manufacturers run by Thomas Bradbury and sons Joseph and Edward, from 1831. Marks registered in 1860, 1906 and 1907.

 **Bennett Bradshaw & Co** Apprenticed to Paul de Lamerie (see p110) in 1721. Marks of 1737 and 1739 record him in partnership with Robert Tyrill.

 **John Bridge** Apprenticed to William Rogers of Bath; became partner to Philip Rundell (see p144 and p111) in 1788. By 1797 they were goldsmiths and jewellers to the king. Bridge registered two marks in 1823, one with a crown. Joined Court in 1831; Prime Warden in 1839. Died 1849.

 **Walter Brind** Apprenticed to John Raynes in 1736 and to his brother, Henry Brind, in 1742. Became a freeman in 1743. Marks recorded in 1749, 1751, 1757 and 1781. Liveried in 1758. Four sons apprenticed to him.

 **Abel Brokesby** Apprenticed to Francis Turner in 1717. Mark recorded in 1727.

**James Brooker**  Mark registered in 1734.

**Robert Brown**  Apprenticed to David Tanqueray in 1723. Registered marks in 1736 and 1739.

**Thomas Bumfriss & Orlando Jackson**  Registered marks as largeworkers in 1766.

**Thomas Burridge**  Marks entered in 1706 and 1720.

**Alice & George Burrows**  Alice was probably the widow of George. Entered marks in partnership with son George in 1801, 1804, 1810 and 1818. Died c1819.

**Robert Burton**  Registered mark as a largeworker in 1758.

**William Burwash**  Registered mark in partnership with Richard Sibley in 1805. Other marks registered alone in 1812 and 1813 (see below).

**William Burwash & Richard Sibley**  Mark registered in 1805. Produced high-quality wares in Regency style (see above).

**Abraham Buteux**  Buteux was Simon Pantin's godson and probably married Pantin's daughter, Elizabeth. Apprenticed to William West. Registered mark in 1721. Best known for plain cups, hollow wares and salvers (see below and p139).

**Elizabeth Buteux**  Daughter of Simon Pantin and widow of Abraham Buteux. Registered mark on husband's death in 1731. Married Benjamin Godfrey and registered second mark as Elizabeth Godfrey (see p129).

**Francis Butty & Nicholas Dumée**  Registered mark in partnership after 1758.

**Elias Cachart**  Prolific maker of spoons and forks. Registered mark in 1742.

**William Cafe**  Brother of John Cafe (see p108), apprenticed to him in 1742 and to Simon Jouet in 1746. Cafe was a prolific maker of cast candlesticks. Registered mark in 1757.

**James Anthony Calame** Registered two marks in 1765. Known for making boxes and watch-cases.

**William Caldecott** Mark as largeworker recorded in 1756.

**Isaac Callard** A spoonmaker who registered New Standard and Sterling marks as a largeworker in 1726 from King Street, St Giles. Subsequent marks registered in 1739, 1747 and 1750.

**Paul Callard** Son of Isaac and Marguerite Callard (see above), born 1724. Registered marks in 1752 and 1759.

**Edward Capper** Registered marks as a smallworker in 1792 and 1813.

**Carrington & Company** The company was first listed as John Carrington in 1873, becoming Carrington & Company c1880. Specialized in wares for the catering trade. The company still survives today. Marks registered from 1895 to 1907.

**John Carter** Maker of candlesticks and salvers. Registered two marks in 1776. He is known to have bought candlesticks made and marked in Sheffield which he overstruck with his own mark.

**Richard Carter, Daniel Smith & Robert Sharp** Registered mark in 1778.

**Benjamin Cartwright** Goldsmith who registered marks in 1732, 1739, 1748 and 1757. Cartwright Snr had a son Benjamin Jnr who was also a silversmith.

**Thomas Causton** Largeworker and possibly pawnbroker. Registered mark in 1731.

**Henry Chawner** Born 1764, only son of Thomas Chawner (see next page). Registered marks in 1786, 1787, and (in partnership with John Emes) 1796. Liveried in 1791. Died 1851.

**Mary Chawner** Widow of William Chawner (see next page). Registered mark as a spoon maker in 1834 and five further marks in 1835.

**Thomas & William Chawner** Brothers working together from c1759 (see below).

**Thomas Chawner** Apprenticed to Ebenezer Coker. Registered several marks in 1773, 1775 and 1783. Liveried in 1771 (see above).

**Charles Chesterman** Apprenticed to George Greenhill Jones. Registered marks in 1741, 1752 and 1771. Son Charles was apprenticed to him.

**Thomas Clark** Apprenticed to Richard Gines in 1719. Registered marks in 1726.

**Alexander Coates & Edward French** Registered mark in 1734.

**Ebenezer Coker** Maker of candlesticks, trays and salvers. Apprenticed to Joseph Smith in 1728. Registered marks in 1738, 1739, 1745, 1751 and some time after 1758. Also registered a mark in partnership with Thomas Hammond c1759.

**William Comyns & Sons** William Comyns established William Comyns & Sons Ltd c1859. Registered first mark in 1859. Sons, Charles Harling Comyns and Richard Harling Comyns, joined c1885. William died in 1916 and Charles in 1925. Formed a limited company in 1930. Richard died in 1953 when the firm was bought by Bernard Copping; it survives today. All marks registered as William Comyns & Sons. Last mark registered in 1905.

**Edward Cooke** Smallworker, apprenticed to Charles Jones in 1713. Registered mark in 1735. Liveried in 1737 and joined the Court of Assistants in 1755.

**Matthew Cooper** Spoon maker. Registered marks in 1725 and 1726.

**John Cotton & Thomas Head** Spoon makers. Registered mark in 1809.

**Augustine Courtauld** Versatile and prolific maker. Apprenticed to Simon Pantin. Registered marks in 1708, 1729 and 1739. Best known work is the State Salt of the City of London of 1730.

**Samuel Courtauld** Maker of rococo-style wares. Son of Augustine Courtauld (see p108), he was born in 1720. Apprenticed to father in 1734. Registered marks in 1746 and 1751. Married Louisa Perina Ogier (see below).

**Louisa Perina Courtauld** Maker of domestic wares decorated with classical details. Daughter of Peter Ogier of Poitou; married to Samuel Courtauld in 1749. Took over the business on his death in 1765. Formed partnership with George Cowles. Unregistered marks date from c1765 and c1768; registered mark dates from 1777. Died 1807 (see also above and below and p108).

**Louisa & Samuel Courtauld** Born 1752, Samuel was son of Louisa and Samuel Courtauld. Mother and son partnership registered mark in 1777. In 1780 their business was taken over by John Henderson. Samuel died in America in 1821 (see also p108 and above).

**Louisa Courtauld & George Cowles** George Cowles was apprenticed to Louisa's husband, Samuel and to Louisa (see above). Registered a mark in partnership c1768. Cowles registered a separate mark in 1777. Died 1811.

**Henry Cowper** Registered two marks as a plateworker in 1782.

**Robert Albin Cox** Maker of general domestic wares including snuff boxes and tea caddies. Apprenticed to Humphrey Payne in 1745 and to John Payne in 1750. Became a freeman in 1752. Registered marks in 1752, 1758 and 1759. Liveried in 1791; elected to Court 1813.

**Joseph Cradock & William Reid** Registered mark in partnership in 1812, 1819 and 1824.

**Ann Craig & John Neville** Makers of rococo-style wares. Recorded marks in 1740 and 1742.

**Sebastian & James Crespell** Huguenot makers, Sebastian and James were probably brothers who may have served apprenticeships with Edward Wakelin. Names appear as suppliers of Wakelin's firm in 1769. Four sons were apprenticed to the trade – André, Sebastian, Honoré and James.

**Paul Crespin** Much acclaimed Huguenot silversmith. Crespin was apprenticed to Jean Pons. First marks date from c1720. Registered many further marks in 1739, 1740 and 1757. Among his most refined and accomplished pieces are a centrepiece in the Royal Collection and a tureen made for the Duke of Somerset in 1741.

**Fenton Creswick & Co** Sheffield-based manufacturers specializing in Sheffield plate, candlesticks and other domestic wares. As T., J. & N. Creswick, registered first mark in 1810. Business was founded by Thomas and James, and Nathaniel joined in 1819. In 1855 the firm became Creswick & Company.

**Mark Cripps** Son of William Cripps (see below). Registered marks in 1767.

**William Cripps** Prolific silversmith who enjoyed considerable success with his rococo-style wares. Apprenticed to David Willaume Jnr in 1731; became a freeman in 1738. Registered marks in 1743, 1746 and 1751. Liveried in 1750.

**Richard Crossley & George Smith** Spoon makers, registered mark together in 1807.

**John Crouch Jnr** Son of goldsmith, John Crouch Snr, to whom he was apprenticed. Registered mark in 1799 as partner with Thomas Hannam and alone in 1808. Liveried in 1829. Died in 1837.

**Robert Cruickshank** Plateworker. Apprenticed to Alexander Johnston in 1759.

**Francis Crump** Plateworker. Apprenticed to Gabriel Sleath in 1726; became a freeman in 1741. Registered marks in 1741, 1745, 1751, 1753 (in partnership with Gabriel Sleath) and 1756.

**Isaac Dalton** Apprenticed to Isaac Davenport in 1711 (see p124). Registered two marks in 1711.

**Thomas & Jabez Daniell** Father and son partnership which dated from c1771. Thomas entered a mark on his own in 1774.

 **Thomas Daniell & John Wall** Registered mark in 1781. Partnership had dissolved by 1782 when Daniell entered a separate mark (see also above).

 **William Darker** Apprenticed to Richard Bayley. Registered marks in 1719, 1720, 1724 and 1731. Liveried in 1725.

 **Burrage Davenport** Active c1776. No recorded marks. Grimwade identifies mark from a mustard pot.

 **Isaac Davenport** London spoon maker. Entered mark in 1697, from Gutter Lane. Two further marks registered, one as a largeworker and one as a smallworker c1697 from Foster Lane.

 **Samuel Davenport** Registered marks in 1786 and, in partnership with Edward Davenport, in 1794. Had a son of the same name who was apprenticed to William Seaman in 1809.

 **Louis Delisle** Registered mark from 1775.

 **John Delmestre** Largeworker, registered mark in 1755.

 **Abraham de Oliveyra** Smallworker, largeworker and engraver who may have trained as a goldsmith and engraver in Holland. Registered marks c1725 and 1739.

 **Thomas Devonshire & William Watkins** Spoon makers, registered two marks in 1756, and one in 1766.

 **James Dixon & Sons** Sheffield-based silversmiths, platers and Britannia metal workers. Started c1806 by James Willis Dixon; registered marks in 1912 and 1914. James registered marks alone in 1873 and 1910.

 **J. W. Dobson** Henry Holmes Dobson and John Wilkinson Dobson founded the business, which became Dobson & Sons, when Henry was joined by his two sons

Thomas William and Henry Holmes Jnr. Firm specialized in making jewellery and silverwares, including the Guernsey Race Cups in 1851. Thomas William and Henry Holmes registered mark in 1877. Thomas William registered marks in his own name for the firm in 1886, 1895 and 1898.

**Jane Dorrell & Richard May** Jane Dorrell was the widow of William (also a silversmith). She registered marks with Richard May (her apprentice) in 1766, 1769 and 1771.

**Louis Dupont** Huguenot silversmith and son of Pierre du Pont, a goldsmith from Poitiers. Registered marks in 1736 from Wardour Street, Soho and 1739 from Compton Street.

**John East** Apprenticed to George Garthorne. Registered marks in 1697 and 1721. Liveried in 1708.

**Elizabeth Eaton** Inherited a prolific firm of silver spoon and fork manufacturers c1845 on death of husband, William (see below). In 1858 her son John joined the firm, which became known as Elizabeth Eaton & Son. Marks registered in 1845, 1847, 1864 and 1858.

**William Eaton** Specialized in spoons. Marks date from 1813, 1824, 1828, 1830, 1834, 1836, 1837 and 1840.

**James Charles Edington** Registered marks date from 1828, 1837, 1845, 1854 and 1856.

**Edward Edwards** Son of John Edwards, silversmith (see below). Apprenticed to John Mewburn. Registered mark in partnership with father in 1811, and two alone in 1816. Edward Edwards' son had same name and registered marks in 1828, 1840 and 1841.

**John Edwards** Apprenticed to Thomas Prichard. Registered marks in partnership with George Pitches in 1723. Further marks registered in 1724, 1739 and 1753. Edwards became Subordinate Goldsmith to the King.

**William Edwards** Registered marks in 1774 and 1778.

**William Edwards** Son of Edward Edwards (see p125). Apprenticed to his father as an engraver. Registered marks in 1800, 1809 and 1823. Liveried in 1846 and died in 1860.

 **John Edwards & George Pitches** Registered two marks in partnership in 1723.

 **Daniel Egan** Early 19th-century Dublin maker of good quality tablewares.

 **William Eley Snr** Apprenticed to William Fearn. Registered mark when in partnership with George Pierrepont in 1777. Other marks registered alone in 1778, 1790 and 1795; registered marks in 1797 and 1802 in partnership with William Fearn, and in 1808 with William Chawner and Fearn; final mark without Chawner was registered 1814. Eley was liveried in 1806 and died in 1824 (see below).

 **William Eley Jnr & William Fearn** William Eley Jnr was son of William Eley Snr (see above) and was apprenticed to his father. Registered marks with William Fearn in 1824 (two), 1825 and 1826.

 **William Elliott** Apprenticed to Richard Gardner. Registered mark in partnership with J. W. Storey in 1809 and alone in 1813.

 **John Emes** Maker of domestic silverwares, especially tea and coffee services. Apprenticed to William Woollett. Registered mark in partnership with Henry Chawner in 1796 and further marks alone in 1798 and 1802. Business taken over by his wife Rebecca and brother William (see below).

 **Rebecca Emes & Edward Barnard** Important Regency silversmiths, supplied wares to Rundell Bridge & Rundell (see p111). Rebecca was the widow of John Emes (see above). After being in partnership with William Emes she registered marks with Edward Barnard (see p116) in 1808, 1818, 1821 and 1825.

 **Thomas England** Goldsmith; apprenticed to John Martin Stocker in 1714 and to Samuel Margas in 1716. Became a freeman in 1728. Two marks, one Sterling and one New Standard, date from 1725. Other marks registered in 1816, 1820 and 1823.

 **Thomas Eustace** Prominent West Country silversmith, apprenticed to Richard Jenkins. Registered mark in 1779. Member of the Exeter Goldsmiths' Company in 1774 and Warden between 1777 and 1779.

 **William Fawdery** Registered marks date from c1697 and 1720. Liveried in 1708.

 **Edward Feline** Apprenticed to Augustine Courtauld in 1709. Registered marks in 1720 and 1739. Liveried in 1731.

 **Fenton Brothers Ltd** Specialist cutlers and sword makers from Sheffield. Business was established by John Frederick Fenton and Frank Fenton c1875. Frank, Samuel and Alfred John Fenton registered marks separately between 1883 and 1888. Firm became Fenton Brothers Ltd in 1896. Supplied ships, hotels and restaurants with their wares.

 **Edward Fernell** Apprenticed to William Grundy in 1762. A mark registered in partnership with Grundy dates from 1779. Subsequent marks were registered alone in 1780, 1781 and (five) in 1787.

 **Bernard Fletcher** Apprenticed to Samuel Lea in 1716. Registered mark in 1725.

 **Andrew Fogelberg & Stephen Gilbert** Registered mark in partnership in 1780. Stephen Gilbert apprenticed to Edward Wakelin and worked in the Wakelin establishment.

 **John Fossey** Son of a draper. Apprenticed to Thomas Tearle in 1724; became a freeman in 1731. Marks date from 1733, 1734 and 1739.

 **Thomas Foster** Smallworker. Marks date from 1769 and 1773.

 **John Fountain** Brother of William Fountain (see p128). Apprenticed to Robert Grace Cleets and Daniel Smith. Registered marks in 1792, 1793 (in partnership with John Beadnell), and  alone in 1797.

**William Fountain** Younger brother of John (see p127). Registered mark in partnership with Pontifex in 1791 and made good quality silver-gilt baskets. Partnership dissolved by 1794 when William Fountain entered a mark alone.

**Charles Fox Jnr** Maker of a wide variety of high quality silverware. Son of Charles Fox Snr. Entered marks in 1822, 1823 and 1838. Different marks used for various types of ware; the number of marks registered reflect the popularity of Fox's products. Regarded as one of the last craftsmen silversmiths before mechanization in the mid-19th century.

**George Fox** Noted English silversmith, probably the son of George Fox of Rundell, Bridge & Rundell. Partner with Charles Fox Jnr (see above) from c1838 when the latter inherited his father's silver works. Renowned for innovative designs.

**Charles Thomas Fox & George Fox** Prolific manufacturing silversmiths working in retrospective styles, established in 1801 by James Turner and Charles Fox Snr. Charles Fox Snr's son (above) entered marks in 1841 and 1843.

**Thomas Freeman & John Marshall** Registered a mark as smallworkers in 1764.

**William Frisbee** Registered mark with John Edwards (see p126) in 1791; another mark of 1792 was recorded alone. Registered mark in partnership with Paul Storr in 1792 (see p112).

**John Frost** Smallworker and largeworker. Apprenticed to Gawen Nash in 1750 and to Thomas Gladwin in 1757. Two marks date from 1757.

**Crispin Fuller** Registered marks date from 1792, 1796 and 1823. Son Jeremiah apprenticed to James Shallis in 1813.

**William Gamble** Largeworker. Apprenticed to John Sutton in 1680; became a freeman in 1688. Mark recorded in 1697.

**Phillip Garden** Goldsmith and jeweller working in the rococo style; apprenticed to

Gawen Nash in 1730. Registered marks in 1738, 1739, 1744, 1748 and 1751. Liveried in 1746; resigned in 1763.

**William Garrard** Largeworker apprenticed to Samuel Laundy in 1729, to Jeffrey Griffith in 1732 and to Ralph Maiden. Registered marks date from 1735, 1739 and 1749.

**George Giles** Smallworker. Registered mark in 1762; recorded in partnership with John Cooper in 1765.

**George Gillingham** Apprenticed to Anthony Nelme in 1692. Marks recorded in 1703, 1718 and 1721.

**Thomas Gilpin** Smallworker and largeworker working in the rococo style. Among his best known works are candlesticks and tureens in the Althorp collection. Served apprenticeship with John Wells in 1720. Registered marks in 1730 and 1739.

**Thomas Gladwin** Largeworker; marks date from 1719 and 1737. Daniel Smith became his apprentice in 1740.

**Samuel Godbehere** Plateworker. Registered marks in 1784 (two), 1786 in partnership with Edward Wigan; 1789, 1792, 1800 in partnership with Edward Wigan and James Bult, as Samuel Godbehere & Company; and in 1818 in partnership with James Bult. Godbehere probably had connections with the City of Bath as he was given power of attorney for the signing of the entry into the register of two Bath goldsmiths, William Bottle and James Burden.

**Philip Goddard** Largeworker and smallworker, apprenticed to Peter White in 1711. Became a freeman in 1720. Registered marks in 1725 and 1738 from Fountain Court, Cheapside.

**Benjamin Godfrey** Largeworker. Married Elizabeth Buteux (see p119) in 1732. Registered marks in 1732 and 1739.

**Benjamin Godwin** Largeworker. Apprenticed to Joseph Clare in 1722 and William Darker in 1727. Registered mark in 1730.

**Richard Gosling** Smallworker. Apprenticed to Matthew Cuthbert in 1712. Registered marks in 1733, 1739 and 1748. Goldsmiths' Company convicted him of counterfeiting marks but the business continued with sons Richard and Joseph.

**James Gould** Candlestick maker, brother of William Gould. Apprenticed to David Green in 1714. Marks recorded in 1722 (one New Standard and one Sterling), c1733, 1739 and 1743.

**William Gould** Candlestick maker, whose most famous work is the Knesworth chandelier made for the Fishmongers' Company in 1752. Apprenticed to his brother James Gould in 1724. Registered marks in 1732, 1734, 1739, 1748 and 1753.

**Henry Greene** Largeworker apprenticed to Thomas Allen in 1693. Registered marks in 1700 and 1720. Liveried in 1708.

**Samuel Green** Apprenticed to Richard Gines in 1714. Became a freeman in 1721. Three marks recorded in 1721, two Sterling and one New Standard.

**William Grundy** Largeworker, apprenticed to Edward Vincent in 1731. Registered marks in 1743, 1748, 1777, and in 1779 in partnership with Edward Fernell (see below).

**William Grundy & Edward Fernell** Fernell was apprenticed to Grundy in 1762. They registered mark in partnership in 1779. Fernell registered a mark on his own in 1780, possibly after Grundy's death (see above).

**Thomas & James Guest & Joseph Cradock** Father and son entered marks in partnership with Joseph Cradock in 1806 and 1808.

**Louis Guichard** Largeworker, possibly of Huguenot descent. Recorded a mark in 1748.

**Nathaniel Gulliver** Apprenticed to Jonathan Newton in 1715, and to Ambrose Stevenson in 1716. Registered mark in 1722.

**Richard Gurney & Co** Largeworker, apprenticed to Richard Bayley in 1717. Became a freeman in 1724. Registered his first mark in partnership with Thomas Cook in 1727. Trading as Richard Gurney & Co the company registered marks in 1734, 1739, 1749 and 1750. Richard's younger brother John was apprenticed to him in 1730.

**William Gwillim & Peter Castle** Gwillim was apprenticed to John Gamon in 1731. Peter Castle was apprenticed to Thomas Ruch in 1734 and became a freeman c1741. They registered a mark in partnership in 1744.

**Martin Hall & Co of Sheffield** Prominent Sheffield manufacturer founded in 1854 by Ebenezer Hall and Robert Martin. Made a wide variety of good quality tablewares.

**William Hall** Apprenticed to Jonathan Bateman in 1787 and to Ann Bateman in 1791. Registered mark in 1795.

**Henry Hallsworth** Prolific producer of candlesticks. Apprenticed to William Cafe in 1762 (see p119). Recorded mark c1769.

**John Hamilton** Prominent early 18th-century Dublin maker of a variety of tablewares including cutlery and plates.

**Lewis Hamon** Maker of rare rococo-style wares. Registered marks in 1736, 1738 and 1739.

**Messrs Hancock & Co** Engraver and silversmith Charles Frederick Hancock worked with Storr and Mortimer until 1843 when he founded his own business. He made presentation pieces and silver sculpture. Hancock & Co is still in business as a retailer.

**Thomas Hannam & John Crouch** Salver, tray and candlestick makers active c1773. Thomas Hannam had previously formed partnership with Richard Mills with whom he registered a mark in 1765.

**Joseph Hardy & Thomas Lowndes** Registered mark in partnership in 1798.

**Harrison Bros & Howson** Sheffield-based manufacturers of domestic wares, cutlery and electroplate, run by James William Harrison, Henry Harrison and William Howson. The business began in 1866. Marks were registered by the partners separately: George in 1896, Henry in 1880 and William in 1866.

**John Harvey** Largeworker. Served apprenticeship under Matthew Judkins; became a freeman in 1737. Registered marks date from 1738, 1739 (two), 1745, 1746, 1748 and 1750.

 **Samuel Harwood** Sheffield manufacturer of spoons and cutlery. Registered marks in 1835 and 1836.

**Charles Hatfield** Silversmith who made high quality pieces that reflect Huguenot designs. Served apprenticeship under Joseph Barbutt and David Williams. Registered marks in 1727 and 1739. Died c1740 and his mother or widow Susannah Hatfield registered a mark.

**Hawksworth, Eyre & Co** Sheffield- and London-based manufacturers of silver and plate. Charles Hawksworth and John Eyre set up the firm in 1852. Marks registered in 1862, 1900 and 1912.

 **Thomas & George Hayter** Thomas, together with son George, registered mark in 1816.

 **Thomas Heming** Maker of high quality silverware. Served apprenticeship under Peter Archambo (see p119). Registered marks in 1745 and c1767. Appointed Principal Goldsmith to the King in 1760 and from this date a crown appeared above his mark until 1782, when he was replaced by Jeffreys & Jones. Liveried in 1763. Earlier pieces are often highly elegant reflecting the influence of Archambo.

 **George Heming & William Chawner** Registered marks in partnership in 1774 and 1781.

 **David Hennell** Largeworker. Apprenticed to Edward Wood in 1728. Registered marks in 1736, 1763 (in partnership with his son)

and 1768. Son Robert was apprenticed to him in 1756. Liveried in 1763 and retired from business in 1773 (see below).

**Robert Hennell** Maker of good quality small domestic silverwares such as baskets, salt cellars and épergnes. Born in 1741, son of David Hennell to whom he was apprenticed in 1756. Registered marks in partnership with father in 1763 and 1768, and alone in 1772 and 1773. By 1795, registered mark in partnership with son David; mark of 1802 was registered with David and a second son, Samuel. Worked until death in 1811, when his son Samuel took over with the registration of his own mark in 1812 (see also p110).

**David and Robert Hennell** Registered mark together in 1763. Marks usually found on fine small silver ware (see above, below and p110).

**Robert, David & Samuel Hennell** David was the son of Robert and brother of Samuel. Apprenticed to father in 1782. Father and sons registered two marks in 1802 (see also above below and p110).

**Robert and Samuel Hennell** Samuel was Robert's son, and registered a mark in partnership with father and his brother David in 1802; mark registered by Samuel and Robert only in 1802 (see also above, below and p110).

**Henry Herbert** Largeworker, possibly of Huguenot origins. Became Subordinate Goldsmith to the King from 1736 to 1740. Registered marks in 1734, 1735, 1739 and 1748.

**Samuel Herbert** Largeworker, maker of pierced baskets and épergnes of Foster Lane. Registered marks in 1747 and, with an unnamed partner, as Samuel Herbert & Co in 1750.

**Lewis Herne & Francis Butty** Registered a mark in partnership as largeworkers in 1757.

**Ann Hill** Registered mark in 1726, from Great Trinity Lane, and a second mark c1735.

**George Hindmarsh** Registered mark in partnership with Robert Abercromby in 1731 (see p114) and alone in 1731, c1736, 1739 and 1753.

**Samuel Hitchcock** Largeworker, apprenticed to John Brace in 1699. Registered marks in 1713, 1720 and 1730. Liveried in 1721 and resigned in 1743.

**Sarah Holaday** Largeworker. Registered mark in 1719 and (Sterling) in 1725.

**William Holmes & Nicholas Dumée** Registered mark in partnership in 1773. Holmes registered marks alone in 1776 and 1792. J. S. Denwall and his son John Gwyn Holmes served as his apprentices.

**John Hopkins** Served as an apprentice under Andrew Archer in 1716 and became a freeman in 1723. Registered two marks, one Sterling and one New Standard, both undated c1720–24.

**Charles Hougham** Plate maker and buckle maker, apprenticed to Henry Corry in 1764. Registered marks in 1769, 1773, 1779, 1785 and seven more marks in 1786.

**Solomon Howland** Apprenticed to Thomas Whipham in 1752 and to Edward Day in 1759. Became a freeman in 1760. Registered two marks in 1760.

**John S. Hunt** Plateworker. A partner in Mortimer & Hunt from 1839 to 1844. Company became Hunt & Roskill when Mortimer retired in 1843. Hunt registered marks in 1839, 1844 and 1855. Marks were registered as Hunt & Roskill Ltd in 1897, 1901 and 1912.

**Samuel Hutton** Largeworker. Apprenticed to Edward Jennings in 1717; freeman in 1724. Marks recorded in 1724, 1725, 1734 and 1740.

**John Hyatt & Charles Semore** Registered mark in partnership in 1757.

**John Jacobs** Largeworker, possibly of Huguenot origin, made baskets, candlesticks and domestic items in rococo style. Registered marks in 1734 and 1739.

**Edward Jay** Largeworker, apprenticed to Gabriel Sleath in 1743. Registered mark in 1757.

**Charles Frederick Kandler** Important maker of the mid-18th century, possibly of German descent. Registered marks as a largeworker in partnership with James Murray in 1727 from Saint Martin's Lane; further marks registered on his own, one undated and others in 1739 and 1768.

**James Keating** Late 18th-century Dublin maker, renowned for boxes.

**David King** Early 18th-century Dublin maker of good-quality ecclesiastic and domestic silverware.

**Jeremiah King** Apprenticed to William Scarlett, became a freeman in 1722. Registered New Standard and Sterling marks in 1723; other marks recorded 1736, 1739, 1743 and 1744.

**William King** Registered marks in 1820, 1826 and 1829.

**Henry Lake** John Elliott Lake & Son was established in 1833 by Henry Lake in Exeter. From 1874 the firm continued under direction of son John Elliot, who was joined by his son John Henry. John Elliott Lake and John Henry Lake registered a mark in 1903.

**George Lambe** Largeworker and maker of flatware, apprenticed to Joseph Barbutt in 1706. Registered a mark in 1713.

**Jane Lambe** Largeworker. Widow of George Lambe (see above). Registered two undated marks c1719–22.

**Edward Lambe** Largeworker. Son of George Lambe. Apprenticed to mother Jane Lambe in 1731. Registered marks in 1740 and 1742. Lambe had two sons John and George who were also silversmiths (see below).

**John Lambe** Spoon maker and watch maker. Son of Edward Lambe (see above). Marks recorded in 1774, 1780, 1782, 1783, 1785, 1788, 1790 and 1791.

**John Lampfert** Spoon maker and largeworker. Registered marks in 1748 and 1749.

**John Langford & John Sebille** Plateworkers. Mark attributed to them found by Chaffers on an inkstand of 1763 seems certain to be theirs because of the combination of their initials. Mark appears mainly on pierced baskets.

**James Langlois** Huguenot silversmith. Registered mark in 1738.

**Louis Laroche** French maker. Registered marks in 1725 and 1739. He was found guilty of counterfeiting marks by the Goldsmiths' Company.

**John Laughlin** Mid-18th-century Dublin maker of a variety of unusual tablewares.

**Samuel Laundy** Largeworker possibly of Huguenot origin. Apprenticed to James Goodwin in 1720. Registered marks in 1727, 1731 (in partnership with Jeffrey Griffith) and alone in 1732.

**Thomas & Daniel Leader** Prominent Sheffield-based silver manufacturers of the early 19th century.

**Abraham Le Francis** Soho-based largeworker. Registered marks c1742 and in 1746 from West Street, Seven Dials.

**Augustin Le Sage** Jeweller, son of John Hugh Le Sage and younger brother of Simon (see below). Mark possibly registered in the middle of the 18th century. A tureen of 1774 bearing his mark carries the golden cup which is also on his father's and brother's marks.

**John Hugh Le Sage** Huguenot silversmith, father of Augustin and Simon (see above and below). Apprenticed to Lewis Curey in 1708. Registered marks in 1718, 1722 and 1739. Liveried in 1740; became Subordinate Goldsmith to the King.

**Simon Le Sage** Son of goldsmith John Hugh Le Sage (see above). Apprenticed to father in 1742 and later to Peter Meure. Registered marks in 1754. Subordinate

Goldsmith to the King from c1754–59 and produced many Royal commissions.

**Charles Leslie** One of the most highly-regarded Dublin makers of the mid-18th century. Mark recorded on cake baskets and tablewares.

**John & Henry Lias** Father and son registered marks as spoon makers in 1818 and 1819.

**John, Henry & Charles Lias** Charles was junior partner to father John and brother Henry. Registered a mark together in 1823.

**John Lingard** Largeworker; apprenticed to William Fawdery in 1709. Registered marks in 1718, 1719 and 1720.

**Seth Lofthouse** Largeworker, apprenticed to William Wakefield in 1676. Recorded mark dates from c1699. Active until c1722.

**Matthew Lofthouse** Apprenticed to George Hanson of the Wax Chandlers' Company in 1689 and made free in 1697. Registered marks in 1705 and 1721.

**Mary Lofthouse** Largeworker. Widow of Matthew or Seth Lofthouse. Registered marks in 1731.

**William Looker** Largeworker; apprenticed to Benjamin Bentley in 1706; became a freeman in 1713. Registered marks in 1713 and 1720.

**Edward Lowe** Smallworker and plateworker. Registered marks in 1760, 1769, 1770, 1771 and 1777.

**Robert Lucas** Largeworker. Registered marks in 1727 and 1739 from Lombard Street and Bow Lane.

**John Ludlow** Largeworker; apprenticed to George Cox in 1706; became a freeman in 1713. Registered marks in 1713 and 1720.

**Jonathan Madden** Registered only known mark in 1702 from Ball Alley, Lombard Street.

**James Maitland** Apprenticed to John Pero in 1718. Registered mark without date c1728.

**Robert Makepeace & Richard Carter** Registered mark together in 1777. In 1778, Richard Carter recorded a new mark as a plateworker.

**Thomas Mann** Largeworker; apprenticed to William Juson in 1706 and to Henry Clark. Registered marks in 1713, 1720, 1729, 1736 and 1739.

**James Manners** Registered marks in 1726, 1734 and 1739. His son James Manners Jnr was also a silversmith, registering a mark in 1744.

**Mappin & Webb** Prominent English engravers, silversmiths and cutlers, still thriving today. Company founded by Joseph Mappin in Sheffield in 1810. Taken over by sons as Mappin Brothers, who later joined with a brother-in-law to become Mappin & Webb. Began producing good quality electroplate silverware in the mid-19th century; now concerned mainly with jewellery. Earlier marks were registered by John Newton Webb and George Webb, plateworkers, in 1866 and 1880. As Mappin & Webb Limited they registered marks in 1899 and 1900.

**Thomas Mercer** Largeworker, apprenticed to William Gardiner in 1722 and then to Aaron Bates in 1728. Registered only mark in 1740.

**George Methuen** Largeworker, who produced good quality salvers and dishes. Registered mark in 1743.

**Nathanial Mills** Prolific Birmingham-based manufacturer of snuff boxes, vinaigrettes, wine labels and other small wares.

**James Mince & William Hodgkins** Plateworkers, registered mark in 1780.

**Thomas Moore** Largeworker of mid-18th century; apprenticed to George Greenhill Jones in 1743. Registered mark in 1750.

**James Morison** Largeworker. Registered mark in 1740. Son Richard was apprenticed to him in 1776, as was William Holinshed in 1780.

**John Motherby** Plateworker, apprenticed to Joseph Barbett. Registered mark in 1719.

**J. R. Neill** Important mid-19th-century Dublin retailer of good-quality silverware.

**Anthony Nelme** Prominent manufacturer of civic regalia, especially maces, and toilet services. His work often reflects the influence of Huguenot design. Mark registered in 1697. Elected Assistant to the Court of Goldsmiths in 1703 and made Warden in 1717 and 1722.

**Francis Nelme** Son of Anthony Nelme (see above) and apprenticed to him in 1712. Marks registered in 1723 and 1739. He was not as successful as his father.

**Hannah Northcote** Born in 1761, the daughter of Simeon Coley, buckle maker, and wife of Thomas Northcote (see below). Registered first mark after husband's death in 1798 and another in 1799. Died in 1831.

**Thomas Northcote** Plateworker and spoon maker. Registered marks in 1776, 1777, 1779, 1782, 1784 (two), and a further four between then and 1794, when he registered a mark in partnership with George Bourne.

**Henry Nutting** Plateworker; apprenticed to Charles Wright in 1782 and Thomas Chawner in 1784. Registered mark in 1796. Later mark registered with Robert Hennell (see p133).

**Isaac D'Olier** Mid-18th-century Dublin maker of good quality spoons, sauceboats and tablewares.

**Francis Pages** Maker of standard domestic wares; apprenticed to David Williams in 1718. Registered marks in 1729 and 1739. Liveried 1737.

**Simon Pantin** Huguenot maker of the early 18th century. Produced considerable quantities of plate. Daughter married Peter

Courtauld. Registered marks as a largeworker in 1701; his son Simon Jnr was also a silversmith.

### Richard Pargeter
Apprenticed to Andrew Archer in 1718 and to James Wilkes in 1724; became a freeman in 1726. Registered marks in 1730, 1737 and 1739. Pargeter was illiterate and signed his name with an 'X'. Liveried in 1737.

### John Parker & Edward Wakelin
Largeworkers. Mark registered c1758. Although Wakelin was in the business first, it is Parker's initials that appear above in their mark, probably indicating seniority in finance rather than skill. The partnership seems to have continued until 1776 when Wakelin took William Taylor as his partner.

### Thomas Parr
Son of Thomas Parr (also a silversmith). Registered marks in 1733 and 1739. Liveried in 1750; joined Court in 1735 and was a Warden from 1771 to 1773.

### A. & F. Parsons (of Edward Tessier)
Arthur Martin Parsons and Frank Herbert Parsons continued the business of Edward Tessier (or Vander & Hedges, as it was also called). Registered marks in 1910 and 1911. The company became Tessiers Ltd in 1920, with the Parsons as first directors. It continues today as one of London's most well-established dealers.

### Humphrey Payne
Largeworker who produced plain domestic wares, particularly cups and tankards. Apprenticed to Roger Grange in 1694; became a freeman in 1701. Registered marks in 1701, 1720 and 1739. Liveried in 1708; became a member of Court in 1734 and was made a Warden from 1747 to 1749.

### John Payne
Son of Humphrey Payne (see above); apprenticed to him in 1733. Registered mark in 1751. Liveried in 1740.

### Thomas & Richard Payne
Plateworkers; sons of John Payne (see above). Registered their mark in partnership in 1777.

### Edmund Pearce
Apprenticed to Henry Beesley in 1693 and to Phillip Rollos in 1697. Registered marks in 1705 and 1720.

**Richard Pearce & George Burrows**
Plateworkers. Registered marks together in 1826 and 1835.

**Wiliam & Robert Peaston** Largeworkers in partnership from 1756 until 1763. Registered mark in 1756.

**Abraham Peterson** Plateworker. Registered first mark in partnership with Peter Podio in 1783, and second alone in 1792 (see p142).

**Phillip Phillis** Largeworker. Registered two marks in 1720. Liveried in 1721.

**S. J. Phillips** Well-known retail business of silversmiths and jewellers founded in 1869 by Solomon Joel. Firm continued by son, Edmund A. Phillips. Mark registered in 1901.

**Thomas Phipps & Edward Robinson**
Thomas was son of James Phipps and apprenticed to him in 1769. Phipps & Robinson entered marks in 1783 and 1789. They were later joined by James Phipps (Thomas's son). Final mark of 1816 was registered by father and son.

**Pezé Pilleau** The son of Pezé Pilleau Snr. Maker of fine quality, often highly original wares. Apprenticed to John Charter in 1710. Registered two marks, undated, between 1720 and 1724 and a third in 1739.

**John Pittar** Late 18th-century Dublin maker of good quality spoons and other wares.

**William Pitts** Plateworker, known for épergnes, baskets and neo-rococo candlesticks. Son of Thomas Phillip; apprenticed to him in 1769. Registered marks in 1781, 1786, 1791 and 1806.

**William Pitts & Joseph Preedy** William Pitts registered mark in partnership with Preedy in 1791. Partnership dissolved by 1799, when Pitts entered mark on his own (see also above).

**William Playfair & William Wilson**
Spoon makers; partners in Playfair Wilson & Co. Registered mark in 1782.

**Charles & John Plumley** Charles registered mark alone in 1830, and with John Plumley in 1822.

**William Plummer** Plateworker known for pierced silverwares such as cake baskets and strainers. Apprenticed to Edward Aldridge in c1746; registered marks in 1755, 1774 and 1789.

**Peter Podio** Plateworker; registered mark in partnership with Abraham Peterson from Primrose Hill in 1783, and alone in 1790 (see p141).

**Thomas Boulton Pratt & Arthur Humphreys** Partners registered mark as plateworkers in 1780. Pratt's son, Thomas, was apprenticed to him in 1785. Two other sons were also silversmiths and served apprenticeship under him.

**Joseph Preedy** Plateworker; apprenticed to Thomas Whipham in 1765 and, in 1766, to William Plummer. Registered first marks alone in 1777, second in partnership with William Pitts in 1791 (see p141) and third alone in 1800.

**John Priest** Specialist candlestick maker; apprenticed to William Gould in 1739. Registered mark as largeworker in 1748.

**William & James Priest** William and James Priest were probably brothers. James Priest was apprenticed to William in 1750. Mark as largeworkers appears from c1764. They are recorded working together until 1773.

**Edwin Charles Purdee** Plateworker. Registered marks in 1876 (two), 1883 and 1895.

**Benjamin Pyne** Important maker of civic and ecclesiastical regalia; apprenticed to George Bowers in 1667. Mark registered in 1696, further mark registered undated. He was Subordinate Goldsmith to the King for the Coronation of George I.

**John Quantock** Specialist candlestick maker of the mid-18th century; apprenticed to James Gould in 1726. Registered marks after 1739 and in 1754.

**Philip Rainaud** Huguenot maker of rare domestic silverware; apprenticed to Pierre Platel (see p111) in 1700. Registered marks in 1708 and 1720. Liveried in 1721.

**Abel Ram** Dublin maker of late 17th century. Known for the high quality of his workmanship; specialized in making communion plate.

**Charles Rawlings & William Summers** Plateworker, particularly associated with high-quality snuffboxes. Registered mark in partnership in 1829 and a further six new marks in 1840.

**Charles Reily & George Storer** Makers of good quality small wares, especially snuff boxes. Registered mark in 1829 and in 1840.

**Isaac Ribouleau** Maker of rare high quality wares; apprenticed to Augustine Courtauld in 1716 (see p121). Entered two marks c1723.

**Richard Richardson** Sheffield manufacturer of silver and electroplate domestic wares. Business established in 1796. Registered mark in 1895.

**George Ridout** Registered his only mark as a largeworker in 1743.

**Roberts & Belk** Sheffield company established in c1809 as Furniss, Pole & Turner. Samuel Roberts and Charles Belk formed partnership in 1885. Samuel retired in 1879 and was succeeded by Charles. The firm became a limited company in 1901 and still exists today. As Samuel Roberts & Charles Belk marks were registered in 1865 and 1878. Marks as Roberts & Belk Ltd were registered in 1906 and 1938.

**Thomas Robins** Maker who specialized in dinner plates and entrée dishes. Apprenticed to cousin John Robins in 1786. Registered mark in 1801. Liveried in 1811; died in 1859.

**John Robinson** Apprenticed to Thomas Bayley in 1727. Registered marks in 1738 and 1739.

**John Roker** Largeworker. Son of Philip Roker (see below); apprenticed to him in 1737. Registered mark in 1743.

 **Philip Roker** Maker of spoons and other wares; apprenticed to Joseph Barbutt, specialist spoon maker in 1707. Registered marks in 1720 and 1739. Sons Matthew and John and wife Elizabeth also silversmiths (see above and below).

 **Matthew Roker** Son of Philip and Elizabeth Roker (see above and below). Registered first mark as a largeworker in 1755. He continued his father's business.

 **Elizabeth Roker** Widow of Philip Roker (see above). Registered mark as a plateworker in 1776.

 **Emick Romer (Emmich Römer)**
Norwegian plateworker working in London from c1758 to 1795. Son of an Oslo goldsmith, Romer, born in 1724, lived in Bragernaes prior to coming to London. Registered mark c1758.

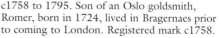

 **Etienne Rongent** Huguenot jeweller and silversmith. Registered only mark as largeworker c1731.

 **Mary Rood** Possibly the widow of James Rood (also a silversmith). Registered two marks as a largeworker in 1721, one Sterling and one New Standard.

 **Alexander Roode** Apprenticed to John Ruslen in 1669. Registered mark in 1697. Liveried in 1687.

 **Gundry Roode** Largeworker of the early 18th century; apprenticed to Alexander Roode (see above). Registered marks in 1710, 1721 and 1737.

 **Richard Rugg** Largeworker; apprenticed to James Gould (see p130) in 1738. Registered marks in 1754 and 1775. Son Richard was apprenticed to him in 1763. Liveried in 1772; died c1795. Mark similar to that of Robert Rew.

 **Philip Rundell** Partner in one of the leading silver manufacturers of the late 18th and early 19th centuries (see p111).

Rundell was apprenticed to William Rogers, jeweller, of Bath and arrived in London c1768. Worked for Theed and Pickett, made a partner with Pickett in 1772 and became sole owner between 1785 and 1786. Took John Bridge as partner in 1788 and nephew Edmund Waller Rundell as partner in 1803, by which time the company had become Rundell, Bridge & Rundell. Registered marks in 1819 and 1822. Appointed Goldsmith and Jeweller to the King in 1797. Retired from his business c1823, when John Bridge registered his own mark.

**Thomas Sadler** Largeworker; apprenticed to Lawrence Cole in 1692. Registered marks in 1701 and c1720. Liveried in 1705.

**Joseph Sanders** Plateworker; apprenticed to Thomas Eweds in 1714, and Joseph Belcher in 1719. Registered marks in 1730 and 1739. Liveried c1727.

**Adey, Joseph & Albert Savory** Albert was the son of Adey and brother of Joseph. Registered marks together in 1833 and 1834. Further marks registered by Albert and Joseph only in 1735, as A. B. Savory & Sons.

**Richard Scarlett** Son of William Scarlett; apprenticed to him in 1710. Registered marks in 1720 and 1723 (see below).

**William Scarlett** Apprenticed to Simon Scott in 1687. Registered marks c1697, 1720, 1722 and 1725.

**John Schofield** Prominent plateworker, known for candlesticks, candelabra and silver-mounted glass. Registered mark in 1776 in partnership with Robert Jones and further marks alone in 1787 and 1778. He also worked for the retailers and royal goldsmiths Jeffreys, Jones & Gilbert.

**William Schofield** Spoon maker; apprenticed to George Grace in 1786. Registered marks in 1820 and 1833.

**John Schuppe** Probably of Dutch origin, particularly known for cow creamers and other small wares. Registered mark as a largeworker in 1753.

**John Scofield** Specialized in candlesticks and candelabra. Registered mark as a plateworker in partnership with Robert Jones in 1776 and further marks alone in 1778 and 1787.

 **Digby Scott & Benjamin Smith** Birmingham-based silversmiths who also worked with Matthew Boulton (see p118). Scott and Smith entered a mark in partnership in 1802 and 1803. In 1807 Smith registered a mark alone.

 **William Shaw** Apprenticed to Edward Holliday in 1715. Registered marks in 1729, 1739 and 1745.

 **William Shaw & William Priest** Makers of coffee pots, tankards and other domestic hollow wares. Registered mark in 1749.

 **Alice Sheene** Widow of Joseph Sheene, silversmith. Mark registered in 1700.

 **Thomas Shermer** Apprenticed to Richard Bayley in 1708. Registered mark in 1717.

 **James Shruder** Maker of rococo-style wares, possibly of German origin. Registered marks in 1737 and 1739.

 **Richard Sibley** Regency maker of high quality wares. Son of John Sibley of Bath; apprenticed to Daniel Smith and in 1791 to Robert Sharp. Registered mark in partnership with Thomas Ellerton in 1803, alone in 1805, in partnership with William Burwash in 1805 and alone in 1812. Liveried in 1811. Had various apprentices, including son Richard in 1821.

 **William Simons** Apprenticed to Richard Hawkins in 1757 and to Robert Salmon, spoon maker. Registered two marks in 1776. In 1776 George Whittingham was apprenticed to him as a spoonmaker.

 **James Slater** Apprenticed to John Ford in 1718, and to Thomas Kidder and John Allbright. Registered mark c1725.

 **Daniel Sleamaker** Apprenticed to Robert Timberley in 1691. Registered marks date from 1701 (in partnership with John Read) and 1704.

### Gabriel Sleath
Maker of a substantial numbers of medium quality domestic hollow wares, such as coffee pots, tankards and cups. Apprenticed to Thomas Cooper in 1691. Registered marks in 1707, 1720, 1739 and 1753 (in partnership with Francis Crump, see below). Liveried in 1712.

### Gabriel Sleath & Francis Crump
Gabriel Sleath and apprentice Francis Crump registered mark in 1753 (see also above).

### William Robert Smiley
Made cutlery, plate and wedding rings, and dealt in secondhand plate. Registered marks in 1842 and 1844, and more as a spoon maker until final one in 1857.

### Daniel Smith & Robert Sharp
Makers of high quality wares in classical style, especially racing cups, candelabra and dinner plates. Registered mark in c1763. Mark registered with a new partner, Richard Carter in 1778, and a further mark without Carter in 1780. May have supplied wares to Parker & Wakelin.

### James Smith
Apprenticed to Peter White in 1710; became a freeman in 1718. Registered marks in 1720 and 1718.

### George Smith
Prolific maker of spoons and other flatwares. Registered marks in 1774, 1775, 1776, 1778, 1780, 1782 and (in partnership with William Fearn) 1786.

### George Smith & Thomas Hayter
Hayter was apprenticed to George Smith in 1782. Registered mark in partnership with Smith's son George in 1792.

### Nathanial Smith & Co
Prominent Sheffield silversmith. Made candlesticks, casters and other domestic wares.

### William Smith Snr
Apprenticed to his father Samuel Smith in 1742; freedom 1749. Registered marks as a smallworker in 1758, 1763, 1764, 1769 and 1774. A parliamentary report of 1773 records that Smith

gave evidence against Sheffield manufacturers from whom he had purchased sub-standard punch ladles. Died c1781.

**William Soame** Apprenticed to Samuel Hitchcock in 1713. Registered two marks in 1723; further marks date from 1732 and 1739.

**Francis Spilsbury Snr** Apprenticed to Richard Green in 1708. Registered marks in 1729 and 1739. Liveried in 1737.

**Francis Spilsbury Jnr** Maker of small domestic wares such as cruets and salts. Son of Francis Spilsbury (see above). Registered mark in 1767. Liveried in 1763.

**Nicholas Sprimont** Important Huguenot maker, Sprimont was born in Liège in 1716. Registered first mark in 1743. In 1748 he became a full-time porcelain manufacturer. Died in 1754. Any surviving marked pieces of his are very rare and were made between 1742 and 1747.

**George Squire** Apprenticed to John Brace in 1699. Registered two marks in 1720.

**Ambrose Stevenson** Apprenticed to father Thomas Stevenson in 1692. Registered marks in 1707 and 1720.

**John Stone** Spoon maker based in Exeter. Registered mark in 1844.

**J. W. Story & W. Elliott** Registered mark as plateworkers in partnership in 1809 (see also p126).

**William Sumner** Apprenticed to Thomas Chawner in 1763. Registered marks in 1775 (in partnership with Richard Crossley), alone in 1776, 1777, 1780, 1782, 1784, and various further marks before his last in 1803. Mary Sumner, his wife, recorded a mark in 1807 when William had probably died (see also below).

**William Sumner & Richard Crossley** Registered mark in 1775 (see also above).

**William Sutton** The brother of James Sutton, also a registered silversmith. Registered two marks in 1784.

**John Swift** Maker of rococo and chinoiserie-decorated domestic wares. Registered marks c1728, 1739, and two in 1757. Son John apprenticed to him in 1750.

 **David Tanqueray** Prominent maker of lavish rococo-style pieces and domestic wares, including a gilt wine cistern of 1718 at Chatsworth. Registered marks in 1713 and 1720.

 **Ann Tanqueray** Widow of David Tanqueray (see above). Registered two marks on the death of her husband c1725. She was probably not a goldsmith herself as wares bearing her mark were clearly made by journeymen she employed.

 **William Tant** Maker of flatwares. Son of a buckle carver. Mark is undated but was probably recorded c1766.

 **John Tayler** Apprenticed to Henry Green in 1714. Registered marks in 1728 and 1734.

 **Joseph Hayes Taylor** Birmingham-based silversmith who produced small items and jewellery. Registered mark in 1880; went out of business in 1888.

 **Samuel Taylor** Maker specializing in tea caddies and sugar bowls, often decorated with floral chasing. Apprenticed to John Newton in 1737. Registered marks in 1744 and 1757.

 **Thomas Tearle** Maker of cups and salvers; apprenticed to Gabriel Sleath in 1707. Registered marks in 1720 and 1739 (see p147).

 **William Theobalds & Lockington Bunn** Registered mark in 1839.

 **Thomas & Co, Bond Street** Retail silversmiths established by John William Thomas in 1759. Francis Bourne Thomas took control c1871 and the name changed to F. B. Thomas & Co. Francis registered first marks in 1874. In 1900 John William Thomas and C. H. Townly took over and continued the business until c1941 when an air raid demolished it. Further marks were registered in 1875 and 1887.

**Elizabeth Tookey** The widow of James Tookey and the mother of Thomas. She was a spoon maker. Her mark would have been entered in part of the register which is now missing and the date is not recorded (see below).

 **James Tookey** Maker of flatwares. Registered marks in 1750 and 1762; liveried in 1758. Married Elizabeth Tookey. Son Thomas served as apprentice in 1766 (see above and below).

 **Thomas Tookey** Son of James Tookey, spoon maker, apprenticed to him in 1766. Registered marks in 1773, 1775, 1779 and 1780.

 **Charles Townsend** Dublin maker of quality wares. Mark recorded on Communion cup and two-handled cup.

 **Tudor & Leader** Prominent Sheffield silversmiths. Made domestic hollow wares such as sauce tureens.

 **John Tuite** Salver maker; apprenticed to John Matthews of Dublin in 1703. Worked in Dublin between 1710 and 1720, where he used a similar mark to the one he later registered in London. Moved to London in 1723 and registered an undated mark c1724 and another in 1739.

 **William Tuite** Registered mark as a largeworker, undated, but between 1755 and 1758.

 **Walter Tweedie** Late 18th-century spoon maker and plateworker. Registered marks in 1775, 1779 and 1781.

 **George Unite** Unite & Sons were established in Birmingham in 1825 by George Unite. In 1852 they were listed in London as silversmiths. Registered marks date from 1886 and 1889.

 **Aymé Videau** Important Huguenot silversmith, especially associated with good quality domestic wares, often decorated with flat chasing. Apprenticed to David Willaume in 1723. Recorded marks date from 1739; an earlier mark is probably missing from the register. Liveried in 1746.

**Edward Vincent** Maker of good quality domestic wares, such as coffee pots, salvers and cups. There is some uncertainty about his identity and he is only identifiable by a mark registered in 1739. Another mark attributed to him dates from c1720.

**Edward Wakelin** Partner in important firm of silversmiths, apprenticed to John le Sage in 1730. By 1747 he had joined George Wickes and registered first mark in 1747 (very similar to that of Wickes). Wakelin took over the business and appointed a new partner, John Parker, c1758. From 1761 the business became Parker & Wakelin Partnership, with Parker as senior partner. Wakelin continued in business until 1777 when his son John and William Taylor joined the firm. Wakelin's work from 1760 to 1770 reflects the influence of French designs (see also p112 and p140).

**John Wakelin** Son of Edward Wakelin (see above) and apprenticed to him in 1766. He became a freeman in 1779. Registered marks with William Taylor in 1776 and 1777; registered mark in partnership with Robert Garrard in 1792.

**James Wakely & Frank Clarke Wheeler** Late 19th-century silversmiths who worked for Henry John Lias & Son. Registered marks in 1896 and 1906.

**Joseph Walker** Prominent early 18th-century Dublin maker of dishes, salvers and communion plate.

**Matthew Walker** Mid-18th-century Dublin maker of good quality tablewares.

**Thomas Walker** Prominent early 18th-century Dublin maker. Registered three marks, all showing initials surmounted by a crown.

**Walker & Hall** Sheffield-based gold and silver workers founded in 1843, initially specializing in electroplate. Sir John Bingham, Hall's nephew, joined and ran the company until his death in 1916, when he was succeeded by Sir Albert Bingham. They registered marks as gold and silver workers in 1903, 1906, 1907 and 1913. The firm had branches throughout the UK. In 1971 they became part of Mappin & Webb, and later British Silverware Limited.

**Thomas Wallis** Apprenticed to Thomas Wallis Snr. Registered marks in 1778; four between 1780 and 1789, and two more in 1792 and 1810 (the last in partnership with Jonathan Hayne).

**Matthew Walsh** Late 18th-century Dublin maker of good quality tablewares.

**Michael Walsh** Late 18th-century Dublin maker of high quality candlesticks and other wares.

**Joseph Ward** Apprenticed to Joseph Slicer. Marks registered c1697 and 1717.

**Benjamin Watts** Spoon maker, apprenticed to Walter Bradley in 1691. Registered marks date from 1698 and 1720.

**Richard Watts** Apprenticed to Christopher Canner. Registered two marks in 1710 and a further one in 1720.

**Weir & Rogers** Late 19th-century Dublin retailers of silverwares.

**Samuel Welder** Maker of domestic hollow wares, especially casters. Apprenticed to Robert Keble in 1707 and became a freeman in 1714. Registered marks 1714, 1717, 1720 and 1729.

**Benjamin West** Apprenticed to James Smith in 1725 and became a freeman in 1733. Registered marks in 1738 and 1739.

**Alderman West & Co** Renowned 19th-century Dublin retailer of a wide range of fine quality silverware.

**M. West & Sons** Top 19th-century Dublin retailer of fine-quality silverware.

**William West** Apprenticed to William Wildboar in 1735. Registered mark in 1738.

**Gervase Wheeler** London agent for the Birmingham jewellers, Ledsam, Vale & Wheeler. Registered mark in 1818 often seen on silver boxes.

**Thomas Whipham** Apprenticed to Thomas Farren in 1728. Registered marks in 1737, 1739 (in partnership with William Williams), 1740, and 1757 (in partnership with Charles Wright). Liveried in 1746.

**Fuller White & John Fray** Mid-18th-century makers of medium quality domestic wares such as cups and coffee pots. Registered mark in 1745. Partnership had dissolved by 1748 when Fray registered a separate mark.

**Samuel & George Whitford** Registered only mark in partnership with Samuel in 1802. Partnership dissolved later the same year, when Samuel recorded the first of several separate marks.

**Christopher & Thomas Wilkes** Barker Thomas was the son of Christopher and apprenticed to William Fearn in 1787. Registered marks in partnership in 1800 and 1804; partnership dissolved by 1805 when Thomas entered a mark alone.

**Denis Wilks** Registered marks in 1737, 1739, 1747 and in 1753 in partnership with John Fray. The partnership had dissolved in 1756, when Fray entered his own mark.

**James Wilks** Registered marks in 1722, c1728, 1739 and 1742.

**David Willaume Snr** Important Huguenot silversmith. Marks registered c1697, 1719 and 1720. Daughter Anne married David Tanqueray (see p149). Patronized by many of the most wealthy members of the aristocracy.

**David Willaume Jnr** Apprenticed to his father, David (see above). Registered marks in 1728 and 1739.

**William Williamson** Mid-18th-century Dublin maker of fine quality silverwares.

**James Willmott** Registered his only mark in 1741.

**Thomas Wimbush** Registered mark in 1828 and in partnership with Henry Hyde in 1834.

**Samuel Wintle** Mark registered in 1778 in partnership with Thomas Wintle, as buckle makers from 2 Blue Coat Building, Butcher Hall Lane. Other marks registered alone date from 1779, 1783 (as a smallworker) and 1792.

**Edward Wood** Specialist maker of salts. Apprenticed to James Roode in 1715; became a freeman in 1722. Registered marks in 1722, 1735 and 1740. David Hennell served as his apprentice in 1728.

**Samuel Wood** Specialist caster and cruet maker. Apprenticed to Thomas Bamford in 1721; became a freeman in 1730. Registered marks in 1733, c1737, 1739, 1754 and 1756.

**Christopher Woods** Registered mark in 1775 as a plateworkcr from King Street, St Ann's.

**William Woodward** Apprenticed to William Pearson in 1719 and to George Wickes in 1722; became a freeman in 1726. Registered marks in 1731 and 1743.

**Charles Wright** Apprenticed to Thomas Whipham in 1747; became a freeman in 1754. Registered mark in partnership with Whipham in 1757. Further marks registered alone in 1775 and 1780. Liveried in 1758; became a member of Court in 1777 and a Warden from 1783 to 1785. Died in 1815.

**John Yapp & John Woodward** Registered mark as plateworkers in 1846. They had a manufactory at 13 Bread Street, Birmingham.

**James Young** Late 18th-century maker of neo-classical silverwares. Registered mark in 1774 in partnership with Orlando Jackson and alone in 1775.

**John Younge & Company** Late 18th-early 19th-century Sheffield maker of candlesticks and other wares.

**Richard Zouch** Apprenticed to Francis Plymley in 1720 and William Darker in 1735; became a freeman in 1737. Registered marks in 1735 and 1739.

# IMPORTANT EUROPEAN MAKERS

**Henry Auguste** Paris silversmith, born 1759, son of Robert-Joseph (see below). Master 1785. Made large impressive tablewares in Empire style, including soup tureens, bowls on stands, ewers, caskets. Died 1816.

**Robert Joseph Auguste** Paris silversmith, born c1730, master 1757. Father of Henry Auguste (see above). Wares include wine coolers, candlesticks, soup tureens, dinner plates. Many pieces made to royal commission; royal clients included Catherine the Great and George III. Died 1805.

**Melchior Bair** Augsburg silversmith, born c1550, master 1576. Made parcel-gilt standing cups in form of fruit. Mark also recorded on wager cups and salts. Died 1634.

**Edmé-Pierre Balzac** Paris silversmith, master 1739. Brother of Jean François Balzac, who was also a prominent silversmith. Mark recorded on covered dishes, candlesticks, flatware and wine coolers. Died c1780.

**Nicholas Besnier** Paris silversmith, master 1714. Silversmith to King Louis XV. Royal commissions included a basin for the Spanish fiancée of the King. Besnier's daughter married Jacques Roettiers (see below). Died 1754.

**Martin Guillaume Biennais** Paris silversmith born 1764. Established a workshop by c1790; became official goldsmith to Napoleon. Made a wide variety of wares such as nécessaires, salvers, tureens, ewers. Retired 1819, died 1843.

**Albrecht Biller** Augsburg silversmith, born 1653. Mark recorded on a variety of small wares, including beakers, cups, and toilet sets. Died 1720.

**Johann Jakob Biller II** Augsburg silversmith, born 1715. Mark recorded on candlesticks, dishes and beakers. Died 1777.

**Thomas Boogaert** Born Utrecht, where he served apprenticeship. Became master 1625 and worked in Amsterdam. Mark recorded on salts and a tazza. Died 1653.

**Daniel Bouman** Amsterdam silversmith, born 1644. Specialized in teapots and sugar bowls. Died 1692.

**Reynier Brandt** Amsterdam silversmith, born 1702, master 1734. Made pierced baskets, tea wares, and salvers. Died 1788.

**Esaias Busch III** Augsburg silversmith, born 1676. Mark recorded on a variety of hollow ware including teapots, dishes, caddies and boxes. Died 1759.

**Joseph-Pierre-Jacques Duguay** Paris silversmith, born 1724, master 1756. Made ewers and basins, cruets and other tablewares. Died 1749.

**Johann Jakob Dulliker** Swiss silversmith working in Berne, born 1731. Mark recorded on bowls and caddies. Died 1810.

**Franssoys Eelioet** Utrecht silversmith, born c1585. Mark, recorded on standing cup, shows stag's antlers. Died 1642.

**Francois-Thomas Germain** Paris silversmith, born 1726, son of Thomas Germain, grandson of Pierre Germain. Took over family business in 1748 as royal silversmith. Commissions included centrepieces for Empress Elizabeth of Russia, and toilet service for the King of Portugal. Became bankrupt in 1765. Died 1791.

**Pierre Germain (le Roman)** Born 1716, master 1744. Not known to be related to more famous Germains. Apprenticed in 1736 to Nicolas Besnier. Published a famous book of designs *Elements d'Orfèvrerie* in 1748. Died 1783.

**Thomas Germain** Paris silversmith, born 1673, eldest of seven children of Pierre. Became silversmith to King Louis XV, also made pieces for King of Portugal, Queen of Spain, wife of Philip V. Died 1748.

**Louis-Joseph Lehendrick** Paris silversmith, apprenticed under Thomas Germain (see above) master 1745. Mark recorded on candlesticks, dishes, coffee pots. Work notable for high quality engraving and chasing and elegant design. Died 1783.

**Alexis Loir III** Paris silversmith, master 1733, mark recorded on dishes and candlesticks of high quality. Died 1775.

 **Jean-Baptiste-Claude Odiot** Paris silversmith, born 1763, master 1785. Work included many large hollow wares including dishes, ewers, vases and bowls. Designs reflected Empire style with motifs such as leopards' heads, swans, rams' heads and classical masks. Died 1850.

 **Jean-Louis-Dieudonne Outrebon** Paris silversmith, master 1772. Made high quality plate and hollow wares, including ewers, dishes, coffee pots and candlesticks.

 **Jan Diederik Pont** Amsterdam silversmith, born 1702, master 1729. Made a variety of small wares including miniature sauceboats, candlesticks, snuffers and boxes. Died 1767.

 **Hendrik Niewenhuys** Amsterdam silversmith, born 1742, master 1763. Made variety of hollow wares including sauce tureens, teapots and boxes. Died 1803.

 **Ritter family** Renowned Nuremburg family of silversmiths whose members included Christoff Ritter I (master 1547), Christoff Ritter II (master 1577), Wolff Christoff Ritter (master 1617), and Jeremias Ritter (master 1605).

 **Jacques Roettiers** Paris silversmith, born 1707, master 1733. Son-in-law of Nicholas Besnier (see above), whose business he ran on his father-in-law's retirement. Father of Jacques Nicolas Roettiers (see below). Roettiers designed and managed a sizeable workshop. Notable commissions include the Berkeley Castle service, probably made for Augustus, son of 3rd Earl of Berkeley. Died 1784.

 **Jacques-Nicolas Roettiers** Paris silversmith, born 1736. Son of Jacques Roettiers; took over his father's business on his retirement in 1772; master 1765. Commissions included a 3,000 piece service ordered by Catherine the Great in 1770 as a gift for Prince Gregory Orloff. Roettiers retired c1777.

**Johannes Schiotling** Amsterdam silversmith, born 1730, master 1762. Made a variety of wares such as cruets, boxes, tea wares and trays, often decorated with classical motifs such as garlands and swags. Died 1799.

**Jan Smit** Amsterdam silversmith, born 1741, master 1769. Made candlesticks, tea wares and sugar bowls. Died 1796.

**Frederik van Strant II** Amsterdam silversmith, born 1709, master 1727. Made miniature tea wares. Nephew of Willem van Strant (see below). Died c1750.

**Willem van Strant** Amsterdam silversmith, born 1682, master 1727. Renowned for his miniature tea wares. Uncle of Frederik van Strant II (see above). Died 1742.

**Johann Andreas Thellott** Augsburg silversmith, born 1655. Renowned for works decorated with elaborate chased relief scenes of mythological or historical subjects. Works include tankards, plaques and sweetmeat dishes. Died 1734.

**Etienne Terroux** Geneva-based silversmith working c1719. Formed partnership with son Jacques. Mark recorded on coffee pots, candlesticks and salvers. Died 1774.

**Christian Van Vianen** Born c1600 in Utrecht, son of Adam van Vianen. Settled in London, where he was employed by Charles I in the decoration of St George's Chapel, Windsor. Made tazzas and dishes that were typically elaborately chased and decorated. Died in London c1667.

**Jan de Vries** Amsterdam silversmith, born 1686, master 1710. Made tea wares. Died 1753.

**Wiener Werkstätte** Viennese workshops established 1903. Association of artist-craftsmen and designers including Josef Hoffmann and Koloman Moser. Made a wide variety of objects intended to combine aesthetics with utility.

# OTHER EUROPEAN MAKERS

**Allain, Henry,** Paris, active c1745, died c1760.
**Allen, Jacques-Louis,** Paris, active c1758, died 1783. **André, David,** Paris, active c1703.
**Andrieux, Jean-Baptiste,** Paris, active c1830.
**Anthiaume, Jacques,** Paris, active mid-18thC.
**Anthiaume, Louis-Julien,** Paris, active c1780–90.
**Aucoc, André,** Paris manufacturer founded 1821.
**Balaine, Charles,** Paris, active c1830.
**Bailly, Antoine,** Paris, active c1750, died 1765.
**Bair, Paulus,** Nuremberg, active 1613.
**Ballin, Claude,** Paris, active c1688, died 1754.
**Balzac, Jean-François,** Paris, active c1749, died c1765.
**Barde, Jean-Daniel,** Geneva, born 1705, active c1730–40, died 1780.
**Barry, Thomas-Michel,** Paris, active c1800.
**Bartermann, Johann I,** Augsburg, born 1661, active 1690–1700, died 1732.
**Bastier, Jean,** Paris, active c1764, died 1711.
**Bataille, Charles-Nicolas,** Paris, active c1740, died 1759.
**Baube, Jean Baptiste,** Tours, active c1725–65.
**Baur, Matthäus II,** Augsburg, active 1680–90, died 1728.
**Bellanger, Joseph,** Paris, active c1725.
**Bellanger, Louis,** Paris, active c1720, died 1755.
**Belleville, Pierre,** Montpellier, active 1736, died 1765.
**Belli, Pietro,** Rome, born c1780, active c1825, died 1828.
**Berger, Louis-Jacques,** Paris, active c1805.
**Berthe, Julien,** Paris, active c1722–55.
**Berthet, Jean-Baptiste-François,** Paris, active early 19thC.
**Bertin, Jean-Baptiste,** Paris, active c1740, died 1771. **Bertin, Nicholas,** Paris, active c1700.
**Bertrand, Jean-Louis,** Metz, active c1735–45.
**Besnier, Jacques,** Paris, active c1720, died 1761.
**Beydel, Jacques Laurent,** Paris, active c1795.
**Bibron, Jean-Pierre,** Paris, active c1800.
**Biller, Albrecht,** Augsburg, born 1653, active 1680–1718, died 1720.
**Biller, Johann Baptist,** Augsburg, active 1637, died 1683.
**Biller, Johan Jakob II,** Augsburg, born 1715, active c1740–70, died 1777.
**Biller, Johann Ludwig I,** Augsburg, born 1658, active 1684–1705, died 1732.
**Böhm, Hermann,** Vienna, active 19thC.
**Boullier, Antoine,** Paris, active c1775–1805.
**Bourgeois, Charles-Louis,** Paris, active c1800.
**Boutheroue-Desmarais, César Charles,** Paris, active c1730, died 1758.
**Bugatti, Carlo,** Italian designer, born 1855, died 1940.
**Bunsen, Frantz Peter,** Hanover, born 1725, active c1790.

**Busch, Esias I,** Augsburg, active 1632, died 1679.
**Cahier, Jean-Charles,** Paris, born 1772,
active early l9thC.
**Cardeilhac,** Paris manufacturer, founded 1802.
**Carron, Jean-François,** Paris, active c1755–1800.
**Cartier,** Paris manufacturer, founded 1859.
**Charvet, Joseph,** Paris, active c1750–60.
**Chayé, Germain,** Paris, active c1755.
**Chéret, Jean-Baptiste-François,** Paris, active c1760.
**Chéret, Pierre-Henry,** Paris, active c1740, died 1787.
**Christofle & Cie,** Paris manufacturer, founded 1805.
**Cortelazzo, Antonio,** Vicenza, born 1819, active
mid-19thC.
**Cousinet, Henry-Nicholas,** Paris, active c1725,
died 1768.
**Crose, Charles-François,** Paris, active c1715.
**Drentwett, Abraham II,** Augsburg, born 1647, active
c1675–1700, died 1729.
**Drentwett, Christian II,** Augsburg, born 1729, active
c1755–80, died 1801.
**Drentwett, Emanuel Abraham,** Augsburg, born 1723,
active c1750, died 1770.
**Drentwett, Gottlieb Christian,** Augsburg, active c1750,
died 1754.
**Durand, Antoine Sebastien,** Paris, active c1740.
**Durand, François,** Paris, active c1830–70.
**Eckloff, Paul,** Königsberg, active 1612.
**Erhard, Johann II,** Augsburg, active c1720–30,
died 1757.
**Erhlen, Jean-Jacques,** Strasbourg, active c1730.
**Fabergé, Peter Carl,** St Petersburg and Moscow,
born 1846, firm closed in 1918.
**Fauche, Jean,** Paris, active c1735.
**Ferrier, René Pierre,** Paris, active c1775.
**Filassier, Antoine,** Paris, active c1705.
**Filassier, Jacques,** Paris, active c1718.
**Giannotti, Angelo,** Rome, born 1798, active c1825,
died 1865.
**Giraud, Jacques-Joseph I,** Marseille, active c1705–50.
**Girschner, Johann Christian,** Augsburg, active c1740–65,
died 1772.
**Gouel, Gilles-Claude,** Paris, active c1730, died 1769.
**Haan, Cornelis de,** The Hague, born 1735, active
c1755–80, died 1788.
**Haan, Marcelus de,** The Hague, born 1707, active
c1730–40, died 1790.
**Hallberg, C. G.,** Stockholm, active 1908.
**Haydt, Balthasar,** Augsburg, active 1645, died 1680.
**Heckell, Michael II,** Augsburg, active c1720,
died 1726.
**Heckenauer, Johann Philipp,** Augsburg, born 1705,
active c1740–60, died 1793.

**Herminotte, Joannes Andreas I,** Maastricht, active c1760–70.**Heuglin, Martin II,** Augsburg, active 1670, died 1675.

**Huguet, Jean-Vincent,** Paris, active c1745.

**Igonet, Sébastien,** Paris, active c1725.

**Imlin, Jean-Louis II,** Strasbourg, active c1720, died 1764.

**Ingermann, Christian Heinrich,** Dresden, active c1730–50.

**Ivanov, Peter,** Moscow, active c1685–1710.

**Jensen, Georg,** Copenhagen, born 1866, founded workshop 1904. Died 1935.

**Johnsen, Niels,** Copenhagen, active c1720–40.

**Keen, Pieter de,** Amsterdam, born 1659, active c1680–1733, died 1742.

**Kilb, Jakob Wilhelm,** Augsburg, active c1770–80, died 1782.

**Klinge, J.,** Breslau, active c1700–30, died 1737.

**Klinkosch, J. C.,** Vienna retailer founded 1797.

**Klosse, Johann Georg,** Augsburg, active c1738–65, died 1766.

**Kopping, Johann Fredrik,** St Petersburg, active c1750, died 1783.

**Kramer, Tobias,** Augsburg, active 1613, died 1634.

**Lakomkin, G.,** Moscow, active c1735–55.

**Lambrecht, Heinrich,** Hamburg, active 1610, died 1628.

**Langlois, Nicolas Martin,** Paris, active c1757.

**Michelson, Anton,** Copenhagen, born 1809, active c1840, died 1877.

**Michelson, Carl,** Copenhagen, continued family business from 1877.

**Lalique, René,** Paris manufacturer born 1860, died 1945.

**Lemon, Erik,** Uppsala, born 1732, active c1760–1800.

**Lemoine, Alexandre Nicolas,** Paris, active c1766.

**Mannlich, Heinrich,** Augsburg, active 1660–70, died 1698.

**Mittnacht, Johann III,** Augsburg, born 1706, active 1735–55, died 1758.

**Möllenborg, Gustav,** Stockholm, active c1897.

**Morel, Jean-Valentin,** Paris, born 1794, active c1830, died 1860.

**Moulineau, Claude-Alexis,** Paris, active c1720, died c1750.

**Niewenhuys, Hendrik,** Amsterdam, born 1742, active c1760–80, died 1803.

**Outrebon, Nicholas II,** Paris, active c1735, died 1779.

**Ovchinnikov,** Moscow manufacturer, founded 1853.

**Pepfenhauser, Johann II,** Augsburg, born 1666, active 1690–1720, died 1754.

**Pontus, Pierre Joseph,** Lille, born 1723, active c1745, died 1784.

**Poppe, Cornelius,** Augsburg, active 1690–1705, died 1723.

**Riel, Reinhold,** Nuremberg, active 1652, died c1685.

**Rigal, François,** Paris, active c1769, died 1788.

**Rohde, Peter II,** Danzig, active 1650, died c1675.

**Puiforcat, Jean,** Paris, 1897–1945.

**Regnard, Louis,** Paris, active c1733, died 1779.

**Reimers the Elder, Johannes Johannessen,** Bergen, active c1660–1710.

**Rehfus, Georg Adam,** Berne, born 1784, active c1805–25, died 1858.

**Satzger, Gottlieb,** Augsburg, active c1745–60, died 1783.

**Schaller, Matthäus,** Augsburg, active 1607, died 1652.

**Schlaubitz, Nathaniel,** Danzig, active 1690–1700, died 1726.

**Simoli, Giuseppe,** Naples, active c1700.

**Solanier, Paul, Augsburg,** born 1635, active 1680–1720, died 1724.

**Sondagh, Rudolph,** Rotterdam, born 1726, active c1745–1800, died 1812.

**Spickerman, Johann Nikolaus,** Augsburg, active c1740–45, died 1747.

**Stapele, François van,** The Hague, active c1720–60, died 1773.

**Stapele, Martinus van,** The Hague, born 1731, active c1757–90, died 1806.

**Stoer the Younger, Thomas,** Nuremberg, active 1629, died c1655.

**Strant, Frederik van II,** Amsterdam, born 1709, active c1730–40, died c1750.

**Straub, Heinrich, Nuremburg,** active 1608, died 1636.

**Treffler, Johann Christoph I,** Augsburg, active 1680–1700, died 1722.

**Trioullier, C,** active c1830.

**Tuillier, Jacques,** The Hague, active c1700–20.

**Valadier, Giuseppe,** Rome, born 1762, active 1785, died 1817.

**Valadier, Luigi,** Rome, born 1726, active c1760, died 1785.

**Vallières, Nicolas-Clement,** Paris, active c1735–75.

**Villeclair, Antoine-Jean de,** Paris, active c1750, died 1764.

**Weiss, Georg Daniel,** Nuremburg, active 1705–15.

**Weiss, Nicholaus,** Nuremberg, born 1544, active 1613, died 1631.

**Wennerwall, Johann,** Gothenburg, active c1740, died 1768.

**Weye, Bernhard Heinrich,** Augsburg, active c1735–65, died 1782.

**Winter, Christian,** Augsburg, born 1661, active 1690–1730, died 1737.

**Wiber, Peter,** Nuremberg, active 1603, died 1641.

**Wolff, Bernt,** Nijmegen, active c1710.

# AMERICAN MAKERS

There was no American equivalent to the comprehensive English hallmarking system, although some American-made pieces may bear State marks (the State of Connecticut, for example, is represented by a staff and three bunches of grapes, a motif which was originally engraved by John Coney for Connecticut's Colonial currency in 1702). Most American silver is, however, marked with a maker's or retailer's mark. Unlike English makers' marks, where initials are nearly always used, many American makers used their whole name within a simple decorative border, and these are usually relatively easily to identify. More recent items may bear the retailer's mark. Listed below are the names and marks of a selection of leading American silversmiths and retailers. Other important makers are listed on pp164–165. Where precise birth or death dates are unknown the dates indicate the years in which the maker is believed to have been active.

### Jeremiah Dummer (1645–1718)

Credited with being the first American-born silversmith. Served his apprenticeship with John Hull in Boston, and later engraved plates for Connecticut's first paper money. Made a large variety of silverwares, many of which survive today. Believed to have introduced the technique of gadrooning (see p88) to American silver c1680.

### Gorham Manufacturing Co (1818–present day)

One of America's most prolific manufacturers of silverware. Company founded by Jabez Gorham (1792–1869) in Providence, Rhode Island. From c1841 mechanical methods of manufacturing increasingly used. In 1868 T. J. Pairpont joined the company and they began marking their products with both a date and trade mark. Earlier silver predominantly influenced by 18th-century French styles; later Art Nouveau and Art Deco styles were adopted.

### Paul Revere Jnr (1735–1818)

Son of Huguenot silversmith, Paul Revere Snr. Renowned for prodigious output and varied life. A dramatic ride to Lexington during the American War of Independence on 19 April 1775 became the subject of a poem by

Longfellow. Prior to the War of Independence, most of Revere's silverware followed simple Georgian styles; later work reflected the influence of English Regency designs.

### Robert Sanderson (1608–93)

After serving his apprenticeship with William Rawlins of London for nine years, Sanderson emigrated to America c1640 and settled in Boston, Massachusets where, along with John Hull (1624–83), he was one of first recorded silversmiths to work in America. Much of his surviving work is ecclesiastical plate.

### Tiffany & Co (1837–present day)

Company founded by Charles Louis Tiffany (1812–1902) and became one of America's largest, most prestigious silver manufacturers. Tiffany opened branch in Pans in 1853 and won an award at the Paris Exhibition of 1867. Among Tiffany's illustrious clientele were Queen Victoria, the Tsar of Russia and the Shah of Persia. The firm also made a large selection of good quality household wares; from the 1890s they also began to produce electroplated wares.

**Anthony, Joseph Jr,** Philadelphia, Pa, 1762–1814.
**Austin, Josiah,** Charlestown or Boston, Mass, c1760–70.
**Ball, Black & Co,** New York, c1850–75.
**Ball, Tompkins & Black,** New York, c1840–50.
**Bard, Conrad,** Philadelphia, Pa, c1825–50.
**Bartlett, Samuel,** Concord or Boston, Mass, 1750–1821.
**Bigelow & Bros,** Boston, Mass, c1840–50.
**Casey, Samuel,** South Kingston, RI, c1753–55.
**Clark, F. H. & Co,** Memphis, Tennessee, c1850–55.
**Coburn, John,** Boston, Mass, 1725–1803.
**Dubois, Tunis, D.,** New York, c1797–99.
**Edwards, Samuel,** Boston, Mass, c1728–30.
**Emery, Stephen,** Boston, Mass, 1725–1801.
**Fans, Charles,** Annapolis, Md, c1785–1800.
**Fans, Hyram,** Annapolis, Md, c1790–1800.
**Fans, William Jr,** Annapolis Md, Norfolk Va, Havana, Cuba, Edenton, NC, 1782–1803.
**Forbes, John W.,** New York, 1810–40.
**Forbes, William,** New York, c1775–1830.
**Fueter, Daniel C,** New York, c1755–1805.
**Gale, William & Son,** New York, c1825–50.

**Gardiner, Baldwin,** Philadelphia, Pa, New York, c1815–40.

**Gelston & Treadwell,** New York, c1835–38.

**Gilbert, William,** New York, c1775–1818.

**Gregg, Hayden & Co,** Charleston, SC, c1845–52.

**Hammersly, Thomas,** New York, 1727–81.

**Harding, Newell,** Haverhill and Boston, Mass, 1796–1862.

**Hastier, John,** New York, d1791.

**Haverstick, William,** Lancaster and Philaelphia, PA, c1780–98.

**Henchman, Daniel,** Boston, Mass, 1730–75.

**Heyer, William B. and Gale,** Jesse, New York, c1800–07.

**Hollingshead, William,** Philadelphia, Pa, c1755–85.

**Holmes, (Homes), William,** Boston, Mass, 1742–1825.

**Jacobi, A.,** Baltimore, Md, c1878–80.

**Jones, Ball & Co.,** Boston, Mass, c1850–52.

**Keyworth, Robert,** Washington DC, c1830–33.

**Kirk Samuel & Sons,** Baltimore, Md, 1845–60.

**Krider, Peter L,** Philadelphia, Pa, c1850–52.

**Lansing, Jacob,** Albany, New York, 1681–1715.

**Le Roux, Bartholomew,** New York, 1681–1767.

**Lincoln & Foss,** Boston, Mass, c1850–2.

**Lownes, Joseph,** Philadelphia, Pa, 1754–1816.

**McMullin, John,** Philadelphia, Pa, 1765–1843.

**Marquand & Co,** New York, c1835–40.

**Monell & Williams,** New York, c1835–40.

**Moore, John C.,** New York, c1832–40.

**Musgrave, James,** Philadelphia, Pa, c1793–1812.

**Otis, Jonathan,** Newport, RI, c1778–80.

**Owen, John Jr,** Philadelphia, Pa, c1804–30.

**Pairpont Manfacturing Co,** New Bedford, Mass, 1880–present.

**Revere, Paul Sr,** Boston, Mass, c1702–54.

**Rich, Obadiah,** Boston, Mass, c1830–50.

**Richarson, Joseph,** Philadelphia, Pa, 1711–85.

**Schanck, John A.,** New York, c1792–97.

**Shreve, Brown & Co,** Boston, Mass, c1856–58.

**Stacy, Philemon Jr,** Boston, Mass, 1704–50.

**Starr, Theodore B.,** New York, c1900.

**Syng, Philip Jr,** Philadelphia, Pa, 1703–89.

**Targee, John & Peter,** New York, 1798–1810.

**Ten Eyck, Barent,** Albany, NY, 1714–93.

**Ten Eyck, Koenraet,** Albany, NY, c1703–50.

**Thomson, William,** New York, c1810–35.

**Waterman,** New York, c1835.

**R. Wallace & Co,** Wallingford, Conn, c1854–56.

**Wilcox & Evertson,** New York, c1892–98.

**Wilson, R & W,** Philadelphia, Pa, c1825–45.

**Wiltberger, Christian,** Philadelphia, Pa, 1766–1851.

**Wishart, Hugh,** New York, c1785–1820.

**Wood & Hughes,** New York, c1845–48.

# GOLD HALLMARKING

Like silver, gold is alloyed in order to harden it. Silver and copper are the main alloys, sometimes used in combination. The alloy will determine the colour of the final metal. Gold alloyed with nickel, for example, will be whiter in tone, whilst a copper alloy will produce a yellower metal.

The standard marks for sterling silver and gold were the same until 1798. In 1300, Edward I laid down the first legal standard of gold as equal to the 'Touch of Pans', or 19⅕ carats of pure gold to 24, a carat being the 24th part weight of the whole – ie an item of gold had to contain a minimum of 19⅕ parts of pure gold per 24. Like the first silver hallmark laid down at the same time, this standard was acknowledged with the leopard's head (see pp6–14). The maker's mark was required from 1363 and a date letter was added in 1578. In 1477 the standard was reduced to 18 carats, which lasted until 1575 when it became 22 carats, a standard that still applies today.

From 1544 the standard mark was altered to a lion passant. When the lower 18 carat standard was readmitted as a legal standard in 1798 it was shown by a crown mark; this remained until 1844 when the crown mark came to be used for both standards.

In 1854, three more standards were established – 15, 12 and 9 carat – and from this time the specific quality was indicated by both a figure and a percentage. Finally, in 1932, the 12 and 15 carat standards were dropped and replaced by the 14 carat standard.

One short-lived mark was the sun, used on 22 carat gold assayed in London between 29 May 1816 and the introduction of the crown in 1844.

## STANDARD MARK

| | To 1974 | 1975–present | foreign imports |
|---|---|---|---|
| 22 carat | ♛ 22 | ♛ 916 | 🛡 916 |
| 18 carat | ♛ 18 | ♛ 750 | 🛡 750 |
| 14 carat | 14 585 | ♛ 585 | 🛡 585 |
| 9 carat | 9 375 | ♛ 375 | ◇ 375 |

Scottish offices used the following marks in the place of the crown:

Edinburgh

Glasgow

## ASSAY OFFICES MARKS

London  Newcastle  Glasgow  Birmingham  Sheffield

Dublin  Chester  York  Exeter  Edinburgh

### FOREIGN PIECES IMPORTED TO BRITAIN

From 1842 imported pieces were assayed and hallmarked. From 1876 the mark included a stamped 'F'. After 1904, each assay office was allocated a special office mark for foreign items to replace the normal office mark.

London  Birmingham  Chester  Sheffield  Edinburgh  Glasgow

# PLATINUM HALLMARKING

Platinum did not come under hallmarking law until as recently as 1973, when the Hallmarking Act introduced a standard of 950 parts per thousand. With effect from 2 January 1975, all platinum wares made in Great Britain that meet this standard have been marked with an orb and cross set within a pentagon. Imported platinum wares bear the figure '950'.

orb  Date letter  Imported mark

### ASSAY OFFICE MARKS

London  Birmingham  Sheffield

# SHEFFIELD PLATE

The craft of covering a base metal with a precious metal, known as close plating, has been practised for centuries. The process involves the application of a thin sheet of, for example, silver to a pre-formed vessel using heat and a hammer. The thickness of this sheet can be minute – the fact that silver can be beaten to a sheet one thousandth of an inch thick, or drawn to a wire of that diameter, gives an indication of its malleability. It was not until the mid-18th century that a commercially viable variation, which became known as Sheffield plate, allowed the large-scale production of plated wares for domestic use.

Sheffield plate was formed with thin sheets of silver and copper annealed together under pressure before being made into the required object. The secret of its success was that it could be used to produce a host of items, from the simplest button to the grandest épergne, at a fraction of the cost of the equivalent made from solid silver.

The development of Sheffield plate is said to have begun in the workshop of one Thomas Bolsover, a Sheffield cutler, while working to repair a knife, the handle of which was part copper, part silver. Bolsover found that under heat and pressure the copper and the silver became inseparable – and he began to use this new material to make small items such as buttons, buckles and novelty wares.

At this time there was considerable development in rolling mills and it was not long before small objects made from Sheffield plate were being manufactured on a large scale. The silver sheeting used was of sterling standard and therefore ideally suitable with its copper core to be raised in the same way as solid silver; and it is common to see hammer marks on the inside of Sheffield-plated coffee pots, tankards and mugs that were made in the 1770s.

The disadvantage of the malleability of Sheffield plate was that the silver and copper sandwich tended to 'fray' at the edges in the course of production. To prevent this from happening and to solidify and mask the border where the copper core was visible, the edge could be cut at an angle and the outer skin of silver rolled over. Alternatively, a wire or thread border, rather like a miniature hosepipe, was cut along its length and applied to the edge.

As fashions changed and designs became more elaborate (especially after 1800), borders of stylized foliate form became the vogue. In order to copy these the Sheffield plateworker stamped out the required pattern for rims, handles and feet in sterling silver and filled the cavities with lead to recreate the effect of a border on a solid silver piece. The filled borders would be applied to the body and secured with a rollover edge. Such rolled edges will be visually apparent as well as being identifiable by touch.

By 1824, Sheffield plate production techniques had advanced to such a degree that the rollover edge and wire became redundant.

Certain characteristics of Sheffield plate can help authentication. On a genuine piece of Sheffield plate, a solid silver plaque was often set into the surface where an engraving might be placed. A coat-of-arms, for example, would be unsightly if the engraver cut through to the layer of copper. Although the standard of silver of the skin and solid plate are the same, the plated area will become visible when breathed upon.

On less important pieces (and certainly on less expensive wares where the underside will not show), only the outer surface had a silver skin, the reverse being tinned. This was a common practice on snuffer trays, chamber candlesticks and the insides of less important pots and jugs.

As might be expected, the designs for Sheffield plate of any period closely followed those on contemporary sterling silver and changed just as rapidly. Therefore shape and decoration are contributory and important guides to dating. After the 1840s and the advent of electroplating, materials other than copper were used as the base body material, the most popular being nickel (a hard white alloy sometimes known as German silver). Britannia metal was also used, as were numerous other alloys which reflected the often impractical side of Victorian inventiveness.

France produced considerable quantities of plate, but their methods of manufacture did not change as rapidly as those in the United Kingdom. Slight differences in style and decoration are usually enough to indicate foreign origin. In England, the greatest areas of production have traditionally been Sheffield and Birmingham, the latter being home to one of the most famous Sheffield plate manufactories, the works of Matthew Boulton. His distinctive mark, comprising two eight-pointed stars, can be found on, for example, candlesticks, épergnes and wine coolers of the finest quality.

Early Sheffield plate was rarely marked, if at all. In 1784 legislation was introduced that allowed for a maker's mark and device, a note of which was to be kept in a register maintained by the Sheffield Assay Office. The practice of marking became more common as the century progressed.

It was not until the late 18th century that a set of marks, almost pseudo-hallmarks, began to appear, which were dangerously similar to those applied to sterling silver. The Plate Assay (Sheffield and Birmingham) Act of 1772 ordered these two assay offices to ensure that no marks applied to plated goods should resemble too closely those on silver.

By the 1820s, makers' marks often consisted of the name in full, split in two to fit a rectangular punch, although initials remained partly in use.

By the 1840s a crown, a fleur-de-lys and other symbols were added, set in a straight line. During the late 19th century the letters E.P.N.S. (electroplated nickel silver) and E.P.B.M. (electroplated Britannia metal) appeared, very often disguised or made to look like hallmarks. However, on closer inspection, there is little danger of confusing these substitutes with sterling silver or Sheffield plate.

| | |
|---|---|
| BOULTON | M. Boulton & Co |
| COPE | C. G. Cope |
| | T. & J. Creswick |
| G·R DIXON'S IMPERIAL | J. Dixon & Sons |
| DIXON&C° | T. Dixon & Co |
| ELL ER BY | W. Ellerby |
| HF | H. Freeth |
| GARNETT | W. Garnett |
| | J. Gilbert |
| HALL | W. Hall |
| IOSᴴ HANCOCK SHEFFIELD. | Joseph Hancock |
| | T. Harwood |
| HOLLAND&C° | H. Holland & Co |
| S H & C° Howard | S. & T. Howard |
| Hutton Hutton | W. Hutton |

W. Hutton

 R. Law

 A. C. Lea

 J. Love & Co

 H. Meredith

 J. Moore

 J. & S Roberts

 Cadman Roberts & Co

 W. Silkirk

 Smith Robarts & Co

Tudor & Leader

 Tudor & Leader

 Hatfield Waterhouse & Co

 J. Watson & Son

 D. Holy Wilkinson & Co

 W. Woodward

 J. Wright & G. Fairburn

 S. & C. Younge & Co

# FAKES & ALTERATIONS

Despite the stringent application of hallmarks to English silver, collectors should be wary of faked and altered wares. All English wrought plate from the 17th, 18th and early 19th centuries, with the exception of very small pieces, should bear the requisite hallmarks, but examples of unmarked antique silver continue to emerge for a large variety of reasons. As from 1 January 1975 (in compliance with the 1973 Hallmarking Act), such pieces may be sold as silver if they were made before 1900 and have not since been altered in any way. However, if an article has had its essential character changed by alteration, for however innocent a reason, it may not legally be sold until the alteration has been regularized by an assay office. Providing all additional parts of a piece are hallmarked at the time of construction, the item will comply with the law. Hallmarks that have been forged or moved from one piece to another are, however, illegal.

The faker of silver articles has to be much more inventive than fakers in other areas of antiques as he has to produce not only the piece but also the hallmark. The hallmarking system is the oldest form of consumer protection, and the assay master is the guardian of honest standards of practice.

The assay master also heads the Antique Plate Committee whose role it is to investigate suspicious wares put up for sale. In the unlikely event of a faked piece escaping the eye of the Antique Plate Committee and being sold at auction, the major auction houses, in order to protect their international reputations, offer a five-year guarantee which gives additional protection. Dissatisfied collectors are also protected by the Trade Descriptions Act.

## Honest Replicas

As collecting silver became increasingly popular, makers saw a market for replica wares. Honest copying became a fashionable activity from the late 18th century. Several large manufacturing silversmiths, such as Garrards and Rundell, Bridge & Rundell, used the designs of the past for their inspiration and began reproducing late 17th-century Baroque-style and mid-18th-century rococo-style pieces. However, providing that a piece bears hallmarks contemporary with its production rather than the period of its style, then it may be termed an 'honest replica' and is not illegal.

## FAKING

There are three types of fake silver:
- articles with forged hallmarks
- articles with transposed hallmarks
- hallmarked pieces that have been altered or incorporated into others.

Fake silverware can therefore be old and improved, or completely new and made to an antique pattern. Without the motives of tax evasion, or the added value of later alteration, the reasons for the out-of-period piece dating from the 17th or 18th century may be difficult to understand. If you come across such a piece, take it to an expert.

## What To Look For

There are several crucial areas where evidence of faking may present itself. The detailing in the construction or decoration may be rather stiff, or the piece may lack the wear that could be expected of an antique. More importantly, look at the proportion; with a little experience collectors will be able to familiarize themselves with the proportions typical of each era of silver manufacture, enabling them to recognise a fake. For example, the bowl of a faked spoon may be too large for most genuine examples of their supposed period.

## Forged Hallmarks

Forged hallmarks are applied to modern sterling silver to pass it off as antique, or to sub-standard metal to make it appear of quality. They can be created in any of three ways – by the use of faked punches, or by either casting or electrotyping a copy of a genuine piece, marks and all. Comparing marks known to be genuine with suspect ones was until recently a fail-safe method of detecting faked punches. However, forgers are becoming increasingly sophisticated and in certain cases microscopic examination is used to determine the authenticity of a dubious mark.

## Transposed Hallmarks

Transposition involves the removal of a hallmark from a small piece, to be inserted into a larger, unassayed item – for example, the marks on the back of a spoon may be cut out and let into the neck of a coffee pot, the solder line often being disguised with repoussé decoration. Such a line may sometimes be made visible by frosting the surface, an effect commonly achieved by breathing on the piece of silver. (Metal is generally colder than breath and silver solder and any other imperfection becomes more apparent through the resulting condensation.) If the results are suspicious, consult an expert. Although marks are occasionally transposed from a genuine antique item to a modern piece, in order to fake age, the majority of examples seen today were applied in the 18th and 19th centuries by 'duty dodgers' (see p13) to avoid the punitive duty placed on silver.

## ALTERED WARES

A general interest in antique silver did not emerge until the latter part of the 19th century, hence the majority of silverware faked or altered for pecuniary gain dates from that period onwards. Before this time an article may have been altered for practical or aesthetic reasons, or because the owner could not afford the cost of remaking. During the 19th century there was the added incentive of 'bringing up to date' inherited plain silver. For example, during the 1850s many 18th-century tankards were made into jugs by adding a spout opposite the handle and the embossing of the baluster body and domed lid with a floral design (see p179).

### The Scratchweight

Many items bear a series of lightly engraved numbers, usually on the underside, that indicate the weight of the item at the time of assay – a small salver engraved '11.2' indicates that the article weighed 11 ounces and 2 pennyweights troy. These numbers enable us to establish whether anything has been added or taken away by simply weighing the piece on a pair of silver scales. Depending on the article, some loss could be accounted for by cleaning, but the loss should not be great and the piece should certainly not be heavier.

### Armorials

It has always been fashionable for families to engrave their coat-of-arms, crest or monogram within a decorative cartouche on a piece of silver, especially on larger items (see Armorials and Cartouches p86). However, from the 1890s fashions changed and an inscription reduced the value of a piece of silver (except where it referred to a prominent or royal personage or event) and it became commonplace to erase the engraved layer of silver. When armorials returned to favour, the arms of a new owner were engraved in the vacated space. During the 1920s, the demand for plain silver returned and sometimes an engraving was removed for a second, or even a third, time. If the silver then became too thin, the upper surface was beaten back again and the resulting dip filled. Differences in colour were sometimes concealed by electroplating the new surface. If an armorial has been removed an irregular dip may be visible and there may also be a discernible variation in the overall colour.

### Later Decoration

Many earlier pieces of silver were altered later to make them more useful or more fashionable. To detect alteration, collectors should form an initial impression based on style, and then ask themselves certain questions.

1. Is the piece fully marked?
2. Are the hallmarks consistent with the initial impression of the date?
3. Are they distorted or in an unusual position?
4. Do any subsidiary pieces lack the correct marks?
5. Are there any signs of repair, such as patches or rough soldering, where newly-made pieces have been attached?

## Candlesticks and Candelabra

Most early candlesticks, until c1770, were made by using the cast method (see p81). By using a genuine candlestick to make a mould, the unscrupulous maker can easily reproduce accurate cast replicas, including marks. The most important thing to remember is that genuine marks will have been struck individually and randomly and will never appear in precisely the same position on any two pieces.

Occasionally marks are removed from less valuable pieces of table silver and 'let in' on the edge of the base of loaded candlesticks. Seams where the hallmark has been applied are usually visible, and the maker's mark will often be that of a spoon maker.

Always examine candelabra carefully; the branches should be marked with date letter, standard, duty, town and maker's mark, depending on their period. Any detachable parts, such as a drip-pan or nozzle, should always be marked with the maker's and duty marks to match the stick. It is quite common to find candelabra with later branches because they were easily mislaid when large sets of candlesticks and candelabra were split up. Replica branches are acceptable provided they are marked accordingly.

Sometimes handles and feet were added to snuffers later. Snuffers are also occasionally transformed into inkstands: silver rings are added to the snuffer tray to form holders for glass inkwells. In such pieces there will be no marks on the added inkwell-holder.

## Cow Creamers and Porringers

The vast majority of 18th-century cow creamers were made by John Schuppe in London between 1750 and 1775 (see p145). Dutch replicas were made from the 1880s onwards and are worth only a fraction of the price of earlier examples. Examples made in the 18th century are clearly identifiable from the hallmarks: if a cow creamer is unmarked or has an unfamiliar mark it is almost certainly a later Continental version and should be valued accordingly.

Porringers of an early 18th-century style are occasionally found made from later Georgian mugs and tankard lids. Such alterations may be detected by signs of distortion on the hallmarks.

## Cream Jugs

In the past cream jugs or boats were often created by converting other less useful objects. Such alterations were not usually intended to deceive, merely to make a more desirable object from a redundant one. The most usual conversions were of caster to cream jug, and punch ladle or brandy saucepan bowl to small cream boat by adding handles and feet and reworking and spreading the lip. Familiarity with correct proportions is the best way of detecting such changes. The marks on conversions of this type may be obscured and when any alteration has involved the use of heat, the silver will have become discoloured.

A silver cream jug.

## Dishes and Plates

Simple circular dinner plates, soup plates and meat dishes were produced in substantial numbers throughout the first half of the 18th century. After c1740, as more elaborate plates with scrolled outlines and gadroon borders became fashionable, many plain services were updated. Plates that were not re-marked are discernible by the distortion apparent in the original marks. Some marks may also have been lost.

During the last century, silver dinner plates were often re-hammered into rose bowls and strawberry dishes. As with other types of alteration, distorted marks will give this away. Occasionally, soup plates were converted into dinner plates by removing the centre, cutting it down, re-hammering and soldering it back into the border. These re-workings can be difficult to identify although an original scratchweight (see p174) may provide one way of checking. Soup plates are usually between 7½% and 15% heavier than dinner plates.

## Sauce Boats and Tureens

Look out for 'let-in' marks on pedestal feet, and make sure a full set of marks appears – otherwise the piece may be a converted liner. Soup tureens made between 1805 and 1840 often had detachable liners, which should have the same set of marks as the tureen except that the town mark (leopard's head or mask in the case of London) will have been omitted.

The faker has in the past found a variety of uses for both the tureen liner and the wine cooler liner. While the former can be turned into baskets, bowls or tureens, the latter can, by the addition of lids, become biscuit barrels or ice buckets.

## Salvers and Trays

Faked tea trays are very unusual; however, when examining a piece pay careful attention to the mark. One which is distorted or struck unusually close to the border may be a sign that the tray has been reshaped or had additions to the borders. Occasionally, tea trays are created from oval salvers or meat dishes to which handles and feet have been added; such handles will usually not match the design of the border as well as they would on a genuine piece.

Plain Georgian salvers were sometimes converted into presentation pieces during the 19th century. If an inscription does not coincide with the mark, or if the style of decoration is not compatible with the date of the salver, then check carefully to see if there are any odd creases or seams which might denote an added border and/or feet. On salvers with borders added at a later date, the additions should have been hallmarked when they were applied, but such marks may be very small and hard to discern.

Tazzas (a type of salver on a raised central foot) were highly fashionable during the late 17th and early 18th century. When such pieces were no longer sought after it was commonplace to remove their central feet and add three or four feet near the borders to convert them into salvers. Such pieces may be spotted because the removed central foot may have left a discernible mark. Occasionally this conversion was reversed and a salver was transformed into a tazza. If the tazza is genuine it should be struck with the correct lion passant or leopard's head erased mark, unless it is a provincial or late example dating from c1750 onwards.

## Spoons and other Table Silver

Although the ordinary spoon, knife and fork are comparatively free from a forger's attention, some of the more expensive rarities and specialist collecting fields are not.

Some types of spoons, such as caddy spoons, have long been popular with collectors. Among the most frequently-seen silver fakes of spoons are marriages between Georgian teaspoon handles (with their marks) and later, elaborate bowls.

Although the conversion of table silver is illegal, it is not against the law to alter and match up patterns without adding extra metal or substantially changing the form. Fiddle pattern (see p102) is not as popular as Old English, so the former is sometimes converted into the latter. Old English pattern in turn is not as sought after as the more decorative later forms of the same design and is sometimes reworked into Old English thread, Feather Edge and Beaded patterns.

From the early years of the 19th century the strawberry became a cultivated fruit, and from c1850 onwards the Victorians were fond of presenting 'berry' (strawberry) spoons. These were usually made from plain earlier spoons embossed with foliage, fruit or flowers. Many of these spoons are marked pre-1800. Unlike other types of later-decorated silver, the value of 'berry' spoons is usually double that of plain spoons.

Sauce ladles have occasionally been treated in a similar fashion to spoons and they are sometimes pierced to form sugar sifters.

Apostle spoons are among the most sought after and most faked types of spoon. They were made over a period of two centuries and were coveted by collectors from the end of the 18th century. Most English-made examples date from the late 16th and 17th centuries. There are various types of fakes; the most frequently seen is where a plain 18th-century spoon is re-worked. Close examination usually reveals a casting from an original.

Other finial spoons such as seal tops and slip tops, as well as lion sejants and maidenheads, are also highly collectable and prone to faking. All such spoons should be carefully examined to see that they have not been altered. Look carefully at the way in which the terminal has been applied. On London spoons the join should be made with a 'V' and on provincial spoons there should be a lap or 'L' Joint.

### Sugar Basins, Argylls and Brandy Saucepans

Early sugar basins were generously proportioned because the unrefined sugar in common usage meant that large basins were required for storage. In later years, as sugar bowls became smaller, early basins were sometimes refashioned as small teapots, with the addition of handles, lids and spouts.

## Tankards

By the late 19th century covered tankards became unfashionable and were frequently changed into jugs or coffee pots. Such conversions were often embellished with Victonan-style decoration.

## Teapots, Stands and Kettles

Teapots were rarely converted but were often updated by the addition of decoration, a new spout, finials and a handle. Tea kettles, like teapots, were often altered, but are not commonly faked. Coffee pots were sometimes changed into teapots at a later date. Such alterations may be detected by distortion of the hallmarks; tea, coffee and hot water urns are occasionally formed from a cup and cover to which is added a tap; alternatively, urns may be converted to cups by the removal of taps. The commonest give-away is a seam disguised with inappropriate chased decoration.

A silver teapot, by William Hunterhand, c1849.

## Wine Funnels

Nowadays, wine funnels are highly sought-after by collectors and rarely tampered with. However, in the past they were subjected to various alterations. The bowls were sometimes used as tea-strainers and by blocking the perforations the bowl could be transformed into a sugar basin or salt cellar. If the spout was replaced by a pedestal foot it could metamorphose into a goblet. A shorter foot and a spout could form a milk jug.

# COLLECTING SILVER

When setting out to buy silver, first establish what you want. Are you looking for a particular mark, or a certain type of candlestick, for example? Decide on a period, a style or a shape you like, and always have a second choice in reserve. Read all you can, especially any history about the item or its design. Then consult dealers and auctioneers. Seek their advice as to prices and availability. It may be at this stage that you have to be less ambitious, but try and get the best example in your price bracket; it is preferable to have a superb cream jug from the 1820s than to have one of the same price but of lesser quality from the 1770s, as quality will always maintain its appeal and, therefore, its value.

A good subject to start a collection is spoons. Spoons have a long history – examples from as far back as the 17th century can still be found – and the myriad types available reflect changing styles throughout the important periods of our social development, as well as providing an ideal way of learning about hallmarks and the manufacture of silver. There is a tremendous variety of spoons from which to choose, from modest teaspoons to serving and basting spoons.

An alternative is to collect silver of a particular period or style, or even from one specific year. Or you may wish to furnish, for example, a table or sideboard in an appropriate style. A further suggestion could be to collect the work of one maker. Whatever your approach, the most important single rule is to collect only that which gives you pleasure each and every time you look at it.

## Remembering Hallmarks

When you are setting out to buy silver, there is a simple method by which to remember the date letter system. Select a letter that is easy to recall – perhaps the initial of your surname – and note its position in the cycle. For example, if you select the letter B, the date letter B was used in 1717, 1737, 1757 etc. As long as you can recognize the shield or background to a date letter, you can pinpoint the cycle and count from your letter to the relevant year without having to count through more than 20 years.

## Caring For Silver

Silver should not be just looked at. It was made to be used and you should not be afraid to do so – silver is difficult to break and a dent, in the hands of an expert, can easily be removed. However, prevention is better than cure, and there are several ways in which to look after silver in order to make damage less likely.

Use it and wash it; never clean it with an abrasive powder or liquid as this will gradually wear away the surface. Tragically, a large amount of 18th-century silverwares have had their definition severely impaired by overzealous butlers and cleaners who used abrasive cleaning agents in the attempt to keep their silver sparkling. If the silver is badly tarnished, seek expert advice before taking any drastic measures. More importantly, if silver is regularly washed with mild soapy water and a soft chamois it will not tarnish but gradually attain a soft mellow look, referred to as a 'skin' in silver parlance.

Never put self-adhesive tape over the hallmarks in order to protect them – there are acids in such tape that do more harm than good. Similarly, never group cutlery with rubber bands, nor store rubber bands inside a silver cup or beaker.

Empty or remove all salt from the proximity of silver when not in use. A grain of salt will burn the surface of silver as seriously as a cigarette will burn wood. Indeed, an open, full salt cellar, placed in a sideboard or cupboard, will cause enormous damage to any silver wares around it, as the salt will permeate the air and deposit itself on every surface.

Nothing graces a table more elegantly than a silver candlestick. However, never remove a candle stub with a sharp, pointed implement, as the silver surface can so easily be scratched. Simply pour a little hot water around the sconce and, as silver conducts heat very effectively, the stub will soon be soft enough to slip out easily. Drops of wax can be removed in the same way from the drip pans and bases.

## Repairs

Never attempt to repair a piece of silver yourself. Serious and illegal damage can result and, while the process may not be complicated, it requires workshop conditions and the knowledge of the expert. A split in an item of silver has to be repaired with silver solder, which can potentially lead to a legal mine field. Any addition to a piece of silver subsequent to its original manufacture requires examination by the Antique Plate Committee at Goldsmiths' Hall (see p172) before it may be sold as a genuine item of sterling silver. This does not mean, of course, that a simple repair to a teapot with a hole in the wrong place means heavy legislative procedures for its continued use. It is only when the object is offered for sale that the problem may arise.

The existence of honest repairs should also be reflected in the price. As a general rule, it is not advisable to buy repaired silver unless the item is the work of a particularly desirable maker or of an exceptionally rare or sought after type.

# GLOSSARY

**Alloy** A mixture of metals in silver, the base metals added to strengthen it.

**Annealing** The process by which silver is heated and then rapidly cooled in order to soften it sufficiently to be workable.

**Applied** Decoration made separately and added, rather than being integral to form.

**Apostle spoon** A silver spoon with a finial moulded as the figure of one of the Apostles; particularly popular in the 16th and 17th century.

**Argyll** A small pot or jug for serving gravy, attributed to the Duke of Argyll in the 18th century. The usual form has a lining or lower section for hot water; another type has a sleeve which contains a heated iron rod. Designs followed fashionable forms from the 1770s until c1830. Examples with their internal insulators removed are occasionally found passed off as bachelor's teapots.

**Armorial** Generally meaning concerning heraldry or heraldic arms, this term is often used loosely to describe a crest or coat-of-arms.

**Assay** The testing of metal to establish its purity.

**Assay Master** The person elected annually to supervise the assay of silver, also called the master of touch or touch warden.

**Baluster** The term describing a double curved form that swells at the base and rises in a concave curve to a narrow stem or neck, popular during the 18th century when all types of domestic wares appeared in baluster form.

**Baroque** A highly ornamental style of architecture and decorative art that flourished in Renaissance Europe from the late 16th century.

**Bayonet fitting** A method of joining covers to bases, particularly of casters, with small lugs twisting into slots, similar in principle to a light bulb fitting.

**Beading** A decorative border of tight beads, either cast and applied, or embossed.

**Bezel** The groove or inner rim of a cover – for example on coffee pots and teapots; often the site of the cover marks.

**Biggin** The small cylindrical coffee or hot water jug with a short spout and domed cover made in the late 18th century.

**Bleeding bowl** A shallow dish or bowl, the lip of which has an indent to accommodate the neck or other part of the human body. Otherwise known as a barber's bowl or shaving bowl.

**Blind caster** A caster with an unpierced, engraved cover, probably used to contain dry mustard.

**Brandy saucepan** Small saucepan, usually with a handle at right angles to the spout. Used for heating brandy, as its name implies.

**Bright-cut** A type of decorative effect achieved by engraving a faceted design that stands out sharply.

**Britannia Standard** The highest quantity of silver used in the making of wrought plate, being 95.84%. The Britannia Standard replaced the sterling standard (92.5%) in 1697 and remained in use until 1720, after which it was an optional extra; it is denoted by marks depicting a lion's head erased and the figure of Britannia.

**Britannia metal** An alloy of tin, antimony and a trace of copper. A popular 19th century pewter substitute, from c1840 it was widely used as a base for electroplating.

**Burnishing** An early method of polishing metals, including silver, by applying friction with a hard tool made of agate to create a lustre.

**Campana** An exaggerated vase shape with a pronounced waist, similar to an upside-down bell.

**Canteen** Originally, a box containing knives, forks and spoons, but often used to denote a full service of cutlery.

**Cartouche** The decorative frame surrounding a coat-of-arms.

**Cast** Of silver, shaped by pouring molten metal into a mould or cast made from sand, plaster, metal or cuttlefish.

**Caster** A container for salt, pepper or sugar, with a pierced cover for sprinkling; those intended for spices were often called muffineers after the popularity of the muffin.

**Chafing dish** Originally a dish with a charcoal burner that kept plates hot, but now applied to a dish used for cooking at the table.

**Chalice** The wine cup used at Christian communion services. Originally of Catholic origin, they had to be used secretly in England during periods of Catholic intolerance. These chalices were often designed to be easily dismantled and hidden, and tend to be incompletely marked.

**Charger** A large circular or oval dish or plate, usually with rich decoration.

**Chasing** The detail on embossed work or cast items, worked with a hammer and punches.

**Chinoiserio** Decoration consisting of naïve figures and scenes in an Oriental style that permeated Europe from the Far East; prevalent in the late-17th century, again in the mid-18th century and continuing through into the 19th century (viz Brighton Pavilion); becoming more naturalistic in later periods.

**Clipping** The unlawful process, common in England until the mid-17th century, whereby a small sliver of silver was pared from the edge of the unmilled coinage.

**Close plating** A method of applying a layer of precious metal foil to steel, sometimes used by cutlers to protect steel knives from staining.

**Commonwealth** The term used to describe the period between 1649 and 1660 when England was ruled by Oliver Cromwell as Lord Protector.

**Crockets** A type of formalized scrolling leaf-shaped carving, usually applied to outer edges of silver decorated with Gothic arches and spires.

**Cruet** A frame for holding casters and condiment bottles at the table.

**Cut-card decoration** Flat shapes of applied silver, mostly in the form of leaves, fleur-de-lys or trefoil, used as decoration and reinforcement, especially on the rims or bases of tea and coffee pots.

**Date letter** The present-day name for the mark first introduced to identify the assay master, depicted by a letter of the alphabet.

**Die-stamping** The production of patterned silver by the use of 'male' and 'female' dies pressed together on either side of sheet silver. Introduced around the mid-18th century, the process facilitated the mass-production of elaborate silver.

**Dish ring** A ring used to keep hot plates away from the polished table surface. Usually with concave sides pierced with animal shapes, dish rings are today given blue glass liners and used as dessert baskets. Also called a pototo ring.

**Display silver** Huge and elaborate articles made with the express purpose of exhibiting the wealth of the owner.

**Drip-pan** The detachable part of a candlestick which contains the candle and catches the drips of wax. The drip-pan fits into the nozzle or sconce.

**Duty dodging** The practice of taking marks from one small assayed piece of silver and inserting them into a much larger piece in order to avoid paying duty on the weight of the larger article; prevalent between 1784 and 1890, when a hefty duty was levied on silver.

**Duty mark** The mark applied to all silverware from 1784 to 1890 (with a few exceptions), representing the sovereign's head, to signify that duty had been paid.

**Electroplating** The application of a layer of pure silver to a base metal (initially copper and later Britannia metal and nickel) using electrolysis, to produce silver plate.

**Electrotyping** A sophisticated development of electroplating that facilitates the accurate imitation of solid objects.

**Embossing** A form of relief decoration worked into the silver from both sides with a hammer and/or punch, leaving a raised pattern.

**Engraving** The incised decoration on metal created without a hammer.

**Epergne** A large and elaborate centrepiece for a table consisting of a central bowl surrounded by several smaller, detachable bowls, used from the mid-18th century for displaying and serving fruit and sweetmeats.

**Erased** The heraldic term meaning literally 'torn off at the shoulders' describes pictorial representations of the head only. Not to be confused with erasure.

**Erasure** The removal of an existing coat-of-arms, crest or engraving, which is sometimes replaced by a new inscription.

**Everted** Outward-turned or flaring of, for example, a rim.

**Ewer** A large, lipped jug, often part of a set with a basin. Prior to the introduction of forks, ewers held water for diners to wash their hands during meals.

**Filigree** Fine openwork silver wire decoration, sometimes in panel form or enhanced with little silver beads.

**Finial** An ornament on top of a spire or gable; hence, the topmost ornament on a piece of silverware (excepting the cover of a cup, which is then called a knop). Also refers to those ends of spoons cast in shapes, such as apostle figures.

**Flagon** A large jug, usually tall and cylindrical, often with religious associations.

**Flat chasing** A variation of the chasing process whereby the decoration appears in low relief.

**Flatware** The term for all flat objects, such as plates and salvers, but more specially applied to tableware without a cutting edge (ie spoons and forks).

**Gadrooning** A repeated border pattern composed of a succession of alternating lobes and flutes, usually curved.

**Gilding** A method of applying a thin layer of gold to silver.

**Goldsmith** Literally a worker in gold, but from earliest times the term also covered silversmiths. The craft of the gold and silversmith rapidly became segregated into two main categories: largeworker and smallworker. Largeworkers made wares of substantial size and included candlestick makers and salver makers. Smallworkers made small wares and included buckle makers, snuff box makers, spoon makers, spectacle makers and watchcase makers.

**Goldsmiths' Company** The craft guilds were established to protect the public and honest tradesmen from fraudsters, and to provide a form of guarantee. By the mid-13th century they had developed into an enormously powerful force. Edward III's Act of 1327 acknowledged the Worshipful Company of Goldsmiths, and bestowed upon them the right to enforce the assay laws.

**Hallmarks** The marks applied to silver to indicate that it has been passed at assay – ie confirmed as having the required minimum silver content. The term derives from Goldsmiths' Hall in London, originally the only place where such marks were struck.

**Hollow wares** Any hollow vessels, jugs, pots or tankards.

**Imported plate** Foreign silver imported in England was originally assayed on arrival, despite bearing the marks of its country of origin. In 1844 the law changed to allow foreign silverware made before 1800 to be imported without having hallmarks added. Post-1800 pieces still had to be assayed at the port of entry. No identifying mark for this later plate was introduced until 1876.

**Improved** Altered at a later date with decoration, a practice common during the 19th century.

**Largeworker** A maker of salvers, trays, candlesticks, plates, dishes, urns, baskets and other wares of a substantial size.

**Loading (or filling)** A system for strengthening and stabilizing pressed sheet silver wares, whereby an iron rod is fixed inside the body using pitch or plaster. Particularly useful in the production of candlesticks made from pressed sheet silver and similar items requiring stability, and less expensive than casting.

**Mantling** The background plumage or drapery against which a coat-of-arms is displayed.

**Milled edge** The system introduced by Charles II whereby the edges of coins were engraved with grooves or a written legend, in order to discourage the widespread and dishonest practice of coin clipping.

**Muffineer** See caster.

**Mug** A drinking vessel without a lid.

**Nickel** Any of various white alloys of copper, zinc and nickel used as a base for coating with silver using the electroplate method.

**Nozzle** That part of a candlestick into which the candle is fitted.

**Pap boat** A small, shallow bowl with a lip, used for feeding children or invalids in the latter half of the 18th century.

**Parcel-gilt** An early means of describing partially gilded.

**Patina** The beautiful, deep, blue-silver lustre that silver acquires with the passage of time and as a result of numerous surface scratches. This effect is lost by machine-polishing.

**Pellet** A small star used as a component of some maker's marks.

**Plate** Originally the term for domestic wares made of silver and gold, the term is now commonly confused with Sheffield plate, leading to the mistaken idea that early wrought plate was plated.

**Plateworker** A general term to describe a silversmith.

**Raising** The process by which a piece of hollow ware is hammered into shape using annealed silver.

**Repoussé** Meaning 'pushed out', a form of embossing, whereby the embossed metal is then chased in order to refine the design.

**Revocation of the Edict of Nantes** The Edict of Nantes, promulgated by Henry IV in 1598, granted freedom of religion to French Protestants. Its Revocation by Louis XIV in 1685 led to hoards of French Protestants fleeing religious persecution and settling in Great Britain, among them large numbers of Huguenot craftsmen, including silversmiths.

**Rococo** An architectural and decorative style that originated in early 18th century France and spread throughout Europe, characterized by elegant, elaborate decoration.

**Salt** The collector's term for a salt cellar.

**Salver** A flat dish, usually with feet, similar to a tray but smaller and without handles.

**Sconce** Variously, the candle socket of any candle holder, a type of bracket candle holder attached to a wall, and a flat candlestick with a handle.

**Scratchweight** A note made of the weight, in ounces and pennyweights troy, of an article as assay, usually hand engraved lightly on the base or reverse.

**Sheet** Sheet silver and sheet metal describing the panels of silver and plate used in the manufacture of silverswares. As distinct from cast silver.

**Sheffield plate (or fused plate)** The fusion of sheet sterling silver and a base metal alloy, usually copper, used as a silver substitute.

**Smallworker** A maker of small wares, such as snuff boxes, buckles, vinaigrettes and wine labels.

**Soy frame** Similar to a cruet, a frame to hold small bottles of sauce.

**Sterling silver** The purity standard for British silver, namely 92.5% pure silver. First set in the reign of Henry II (1154–89) it is still in use today.

**Strapwork** A decorative method probably brought to England by Huguenot craftsmen and consisting of interlacing straps or bands of ornament. These were originally engraved but, by the end of the 17th century, cast and applied in a more elaborate form. Also describes a type of formal design.

**Tankard** Large mug with a hinged lid and thumbpiece, used for drinking beer.

**Tazza** A type of salver on a raised central stand.

**Thumbpiece** The flange attached to a hinged lid which, when pressed by the thumb, raises the lid.

**Touch** Originally, the test by touchstone to discover the purity of metal before receiving the mark of the assay office.

**Touchstone** A hard, dark, siliceous stone (perhaps basalt or jasper) used to test the quality of gold and silver.

**Trefid** A 17th-century spoon, the handle of which terminates as a bud shape, usually cleft into a central stem and two lobes.

**Trefoil** The term describing decorative motifs with three leaves or lobes.

**Troy** A system to measure the weight of precious stones and metals first used at Troyes in France. The system is based on the weight of a grain. 24 grains = 1 pennyweight; 20 pennyweights = 1 troy ounce; 12 ounces = 1 troy pound.

**Worshipful Company of Goldsmiths** The ancient company of the City of London established to represent those involved in gold and silversmithing.

**Wrought plate** The ancient and general term for all silverware and gold made by hand.

# GENERAL INDEX

# ACKNOWLEDGMENTS

Thanks are due to the following for their help in the preparation of this book:

**Giorgio Busetto**
**www.silvercollection.it**
giobuse1@tin.it

**Graham Hodges**
**www.silversugartongs.com**
☎ 01225 755604

**Gary Bottomley**
**www.antiquesilverspoons.com**
rbeaultd@btopenworld.com
*Telephone number only available after contact via email has been gained*

**Sally Bagott**
The Birmingham Assay Office
info@theassayoffice.co.uk
☎ 0121 236 6951

**Daniel Bexfield Antiques**
**www.bexfield.co.uk**
antiques@bexfield.co.uk
☎ 020 7491 1720

**I. Franks – Daniel Franks**
**www.ifranks.com**
☎ 020 7242 4035

**Sanda Lipton**
☎ 020 7431 0866
🖷 020 7431 3224

**Mary Cooke Antiques Ltd.**
**www.marycooke.co.uk**
silver@marycooke.co.uk
☎ 020 8876 5777

**Brayhawks Ltd.**
**www.brayhawks.co.uk**
brayhawks@onetel.com
☎ 01959 561222

**Stephen Kalms**
**www.kalmsantiques.com**
stephen@kalmsantiques.com
☎ 020 7430 1254
🖷 020 7405 6206

**Koopman Rare Art**
**– Timo Koopman**
**www.rareartlondon.com**
timo@rareartlondon.com
☎ 020 7242 7624